THE SACRAMENT OF THE LORD'S SUPPER
In the Fullness of the Gospel

THE SACRAMENT OF THE LORD'S SUPPER
In the Fullness of the Gospel

By George A. Njeim

HERALD PUBLISHING HOUSE
Independence, Missouri

Library of Congress Cataloging in Publication Data

Njeim, George A
  The sacrament of the Lord's Supper.

  1. Lord's Supper—Mormonism.   2. Reorganized Church of Jesus Christ
of Latter Day Saints—Doctrinal and controversial works.   I. Title.
BX8655.2.N56   264'.09'3   77-7649
ISBN 0-8309-0182-5

Printed in the United States of America

CONTENTS

ACKNOWLEDGMENTS

A work like this, and at this particular time of my life, is not accomplished without the gracious help of others. Soon after I started assembling the material for this volume my cataracts reached the place where I found it agonizing to read typed material. I acknowledge with deep appreciation the help of Elder Novy Bowman who put the first three chapters in large, bold type so I could read and make the needed changes. My thanks also go to my son-in-law, Elder Michael Coulson. During my surgery and convalescence I was not able to resume my writing. This was a period of discouragement and frustration. During this time we visited with our daughter and her family in Calgary, and I took with me what was already finished of the work. Michael, a recent convert to the church, had had one year of theological studies at the University of Durham before taking up his present discipline. He was most qualified to pass critical judgment on the work and to tell me where I was wrong. Instead, his enthusiastic support was infectious. He even was kind enough to obtain source material to augment references I had already quoted which were not available in my area.

I wish also to acknowledge the valuable help of Elder Leslie Flowers (former assistant editor of *Vision*, a 1929-1932 church periodical) who had just been retired from his editorial work in the offices of the state of Michigan. He was kind enough to read the manuscript, check references, and do editorial corrections. I also appreciate the word of "commendation" from President W. Wallace Smith, who took time to read the manuscript before the foreword was written. Subsequent to this he submitted the work to others (whose names I do not know) for their evaluation. The last one to read the manuscript, and whose opinion I highly respect, was Elder F. Henry Edwards. These brethren offered helpful suggestions for the improvement of the work, and where possible some of these adjustments were added to the foreword. It should be made clear at this point, however, that the work is mine, and I am solely responsible for any mistakes and the accuracy of the account.

A final word of appreciation goes to Pam Jenks who typed the manuscript in its final form.

Though this work bears my name from inception to finish, I would not ignore the moral, physical, and spiritual support I received from Vera, my companion for forty years. Together we studied the material as I wrote it. She was horrified at the extent of vital contradictions in the New Testament account, but she was more than delighted at the discovery of the answers in the Book of Mormon. She was always watching for theological terms and big words and suggested their removal. Her sacrificial devotion to her faith, husband, and children were unequaled in my judgment. Though she appeared in declining health, I never thought of her sudden death. She showed more than ordinary interest in the last chapter as together we studied the outline. Also she was most impatient at the discovery that I was taking my time in writing it. Almost a month before her demise, and when the manuscript was not being discussed, she called me to her bedside and said, "George, see to it that this manuscript is published, regardless of who may publish it and the cost it may entail." Did she have a premonition of her death? I believe she did. If so—and to use a favorite quote of hers—she preceded me "to meet," again, "before the pleasing bar of the great Jehovah, the eternal judge of both quick and dead." This is her work as much as it is mine.

INTRODUCTION

It has been evident for quite some time that our Christian faith is going through a period of examination, and one of the institutions being examined is the subject of this thesis—the Lord's Supper. In spite of the many theological attitudes and changes regarding it, the Supper originally rested on the authority of Christ. During the last two hundred years of critical study, however, the validity of the meal has been in question, and its theology is undergoing a process of change. The first questioning began with Protestant theologians and affected only that community. Following this, Roman Catholic theologians became involved in the search. Old beliefs were challenged by newer and unexpected evidences of contradictions in the gospels. Education of the masses added fuel to the debate, increasing the suffering of the faith. Heroic measures are being undertaken by dedicated and God-fearing students to stabilize the loss. Due to the unprecedented and fast changes taking place in the economic, social, ideological, and environmental arenas of life, however, the majority are impatient with spiritual considerations, the fundamental record (New Testament) of which appears subject to question.

The peculiar feature of this stand is that it is a reversal of other historical events which developed when man was facing fast change and extreme danger. As the Jews found themselves helpless against the onslaught of the Roman legions, they resorted to the dwelling place of God—the temple—and died by the thousands. When the barbarians invaded Rome the citizenry turned to the church. When the great depression gripped the industrialized world in the thirties, a noted psychologist, Henry Charles Link, wrote a book titled *The Return to Religion.* After Niemoeller saw the havoc accomplished by his submarines on allied shipping and witnessed the destruction by warring nations he discarded his naval uniform, studied religion, and became known as Pastor Niemoeller. Such comparable return to organized Christianity does not appear to be taking place. Instead, numbers of the young are attracted to newer cults of oriental origin—Zen Buddhism, Transcendental Meditation, and the Unification Church. Others have been congregating around subcults distinguished by long hair, bizarre clothing, communal living, the use of mind-altering drugs, and—in extreme cases—Satan worship.

An Unresolved Issue

The baffling thing is that this discontent with Christian institutions in general and the Lord's Supper in particular has reached us as a church. We claim divine revelation, and our position on the Lord's Supper is clear. In spite of this, for the last four years we have been debating whether we are close or open Communionists. From my limited observation I have come to the conclusion that, whichever side we are on, we lack awareness of the background of the position we take. To a large extent we depend on our traditions or a limited knowledge of the development which brought the position into focus. A discussion like this is always

12

inconclusive and often results in hard feelings. When in despair, we throw the problem to the First Presidency and World Conference to decide the issue. Three of the presidents of the church answered the question by supporting close Communion, but apparently this was unsatisfactory or the question would not continue to come back. After some inconclusive study, the Conference debated the issue in 1974, but I suspect the debators presented their point of view without sufficient reasoning going back to a central authority to which the positive and negative would bow in humble submission.

Those standing for close Communion depend on the account of the Lord's Supper in the Book of Mormon. This is well known to those who hold to open Communion but consider the Scripture as being insufficient. To a few of this group the Book of Mormon account is an outdated exhibit. They do not reject the revelatory power behind it but consider the revelation as dated, limiting it to the nineteenth century. They have the same attitude toward the instruction given in the Doctrine and Covenants. On the contrary, those believing in close Communion consider the message of the book in general and the account of the Lord's Supper in particular as being timeless.

When an impasse like this is reached, debate becomes futile. What is needed is evidence to prove a position. Our forefathers in the church depended on faith to sustain their belief. The proof came from their own deep feelings; we just believe. When additional evidence was needed they resorted to the Old and New Testaments. This does not generally hold true today, when psychology is revered and the Scriptures are questioned.

Something has been going on in the theological world of which the majority of us in the church are not sufficiently aware; that something is *criticism*. There are various types, but in this study they will be referred to as "higher criticisms." The result of these has been the discovery that the New Testament record is deficient, and the picture it gives us of Christ and his teachings is somewhat blurred. What to our forefathers was crystal clear is foggy to many of us. When the Christians of the differing sects argued a doctrinal issue, they based their positions on biblical understanding of the doctrine. Now we know that some of these are not as clear to us as they were to our predecessors—including the Lord's Supper. Many knowledgeable students accommodate themselves to the new "reality." This is one of the reasons behind the ecumenical movement.

As we enter into the study of the Lord's Supper in the New Testament some of us may become disturbed by the findings of the critical movement. Higher criticism, however, is not an evil to be shunned—certainly not by believers in the Restoration. Since the aim of some of the higher critics is discovery of the truth, their findings ought to be utilized. There are those who may be termed materialistic critics, but the majority are God-fearing men who are trying to find meaning or answers to the questions and contradictions. The second chapter of this book is devoted to these findings and reveals that the belief which we have accepted on faith—but may never have been able to critically defend—is true, namely " . . . that there are many plain and precious things taken away from the book, which is the book of the Lamb of God." (This statement appeared in the Book of Mormon before the modern art of higher criticism became known.)

It is lamentable that as a church we have not given the findings of higher criticism more recognition. My emphasis on the discoveries of this movement regarding the deficiency in the gospel text may come as a shock to some. This should not be. If the critic discovered what the Lord had already told us about the mutilation in the gospel, may he not have given the answer to correct these deficiencies in the same record? I believe he has— and the Book of Mormon gives us the answer.

The issue is not so much open or close Communion as it is proof of the position taken. Those holding to the belief in open Communion have, in my judgment, failed to offer sufficient proof that the message of the Book of Mormon on the Lord's Supper is limited to the nineteenth century. The same holds true of those believing in close Communion. They ignore the root of the problem, depending on faith in the Book of Mormon without validating the account. I believe there are revelations which may be called timely (some appear in the Doctrine and Covenants), but the revelation of Christ in the Book of Mormon is timeless and eternal. The same is true of the sacrament of the Lord's Supper and other principles of the gospel.

Why the Book of Mormon

In spite of all the problems modern students find in the coming forth of the book (such as angelic ministry, the Urim and Thummim, the method of translation, and poor syntax), this record remains the basic revelation of

Latter Day Saintism. The church was built on it. Because of it Joseph Smith was recognized as a prophet. The church which we call prophetic today would lose its designation if its first prophet was discovered to have been in error in bringing forth the Book of Mormon. Our belief in continuing revelation would also suffer if the first revelation was found false. If the foundation is found to be faulty, the structure erected on it would ultimately fall.

Another reason is what appear to be fantastic assumptions. The Nephite section of the book is woven around the miraculous selection of two families of the house of Israel in Palestine and their divine guidance across the ocean to the Western Hemisphere. With them they brought the records of their forefathers. Later they were joined by another group of refugees from the same locality, subsequent to the Babylonian conquest. The prophetic hope of a Messiah appears to be paramount in their teachings. A Christology was developed which had no parallel among those who were left in Palestine. After his ministry, death, and resurrection in Jerusalem, Jesus appeared physically to these people, taught them, chose and ordained twelve disciples, established the church, and served the Lord's Supper. Hence, the gospel was preached in America as it was preached in Palestine.

The preamble of the book states its purpose in these succinct words:

...To shew unto the remnant of the house of Israel what great things the Lord hath done for their fathers...and also to the convincing of the Jew and Gentile that Jesus is the Christ, the Eternal God, manifesting himself unto all nations.

The statement then concludes with what may appear as

an escape clause: "...If there are faults [in the Book] they are the faults of men...."

In addition to this the book explains the need for the fullness of the gospel. The sacred word came from the Jews:

...And when it proceeded from the mouth of a Jew [presumably Jesus] it contained the plainness of the gospel of the Lord, of whom the twelve apostles bear record....After they go forth by the hand of the twelve apostles of the Lamb, from the Jews unto the Gentiles, thou seest the foundation of a great and abominable church, which is most abominable above all other churches; for behold, they have taken away from the gospel of the Lamb many parts which are plain and most precious; and also many covenants of the Lord have they taken away.

Because of this tampering with the sacred text, "many do stumble" (I Nephi 3:161-175).

These claims were usually rejected as absurd assumptions. To our forefathers, however, they were the gospel truth. To us they are extremely bewildering. Perhaps this is why there is a lack of emphasis among some of us on the message of the book. Ignoring the problem, however, does not solve it; it simply becomes compounded.

Out of these claims there emerge two significantly outstanding conclusions. First, there is the *deficiency* of the gospel as we know it. Second, there is the *fullness of the gospel* which the book claims to supply. These two points will play a major role in the investigation which follows.

The Abominable Church

The identity of the abominable church which has caused such drastic changes in the gospel has been a source of considerable speculation, and some have doubted the divinity of the statement. I, too, have considered the possibility of its human source. Some years back, however, after I read Rudolf Bultmann's *Primitive Christianity*, I entertained the idea that Christian Gnosticism may be the answer to this "abomination." All that was known of the movement at the time is what was transmitted by the early Christian fathers. German students devoted much of their energies to its study in the nineteenth century. Church historians give it slight mention but no elaboration. Marcion and Valentinus appear to have been its greatest advocates. Both of them are mentioned by Eusebius, who makes it appear that the church triumphed over this heresy by the end of the second and early part of the third century (Book V, Chap. 11). According to recent discoveries, however, the conflict over this abomination went on longer than that.

Origin of Gnosticism

Originally Gnosticism was an Eastern philosophy which invaded Western thought. It combined Persian and, some think, Hindu philosophies which ultimately influenced the Greeks. In return this influence reached Judaism and then Christianity. Simon Magus, the man who attempted to purchase the Holy Ghost from Peter, appears to have been its Christian founder (Acts 8:9-21). If so, magic was combined with its teachings. Gnostics believed in two gods—the god of light and the god of darkness. Light was good, and darkness was evil. They believed that man was also composed of two things—flesh and soul. The flesh was evil imprisoning the soul. Out of this belief came the idea of redemption and salvation from the flesh and the world of darkness. In order for the soul to escape from this evil world it

18

had to learn the secret of salvation. The Greek word for this process was *gnosis*—knowledge. The ultimate hope of the soul was to reach the god of light, but the course it had to take was obstructed by myriads of angels, demons, and demiurges. First it was thought that the seven planets guarded the entrance to the world of light. Man had to know the password in order to get by them. Later on the numbers of the guards increased, and the time to achieve the goal took aeons.

The Gnostic Heresy

The most ingenious thing about Gnostics is the manner by which they adapted Christian teachings to their aim. By doing this they created the greatest heresy on record. As *gnosis* became knowledge to the Greeks, to the Gnostic Christians it became revelation. First, the unbegotten Father (God of light) was opposed by the god of darkness and his angels. Sometimes they appeared to have proceeded from him, yet in other teachings they appeared to have had an independent origin. They were believed to be the creators of this world and to have control of it. The God of the Old Testament was one of them. According to some, prophecy came from the world makers, the Jewish god being the supreme. Second, Jesus and other souls remained pure in the knowledge of the unbegotten Father. Because of this purity, Jesus had the power to destroy the Jewish god. For this reason the Old Testament and the Mosaic law written in it had to go.

The most influential and yet dangerous of the early writers of Christian Gnosticism was Marcion. He did not reject the historicity of the Old Testament but rejected the allegorical references in it which connected the Messiah with the person of Jesus. Of particular interest were his views on the gospels. The Old Testament canon was already established, so another was needed to establish the New Testament. Out of the existing but scattered Christian Gospels of the day he chose the gospel according to Luke as being authentic. He believed the others (how many we do not know) were forged. Some of Paul's writings were chosen; others were rejected. These made the canon of his new testament. Even this had to be amended in order to remove from it any connection with Judaism. The genealogy of the Lord mentioned by Luke had to be removed. So were other references to the prophetic coming of the Messiah. In addition to this he wrote the gospel which bears his name. All of this happened before orthodox believers awakened to the fact that an orthodox canon had to be assembled.

Like the other Gnostics before him Marcion believed in the two-god system—the "just god" of the Old Testament and the "good god" of the New Testament who is Jesus. He rejected the Old Testament God who required eye for eye and tooth for tooth. The New Testament God required faith and offered his grace. Remission of sins and atonement meant nothing to him. Oregin, denouncing these claims, wrote: "This God, just and good, the Father of our Lord Jesus Christ, has himself given the law and the prophets and the gospels, he who is the God of the Old and New Testament" (*The Gnostic Religion*, by Hans Jonas, Beacon Press, Boston, p. 164). This is simply an example of the conflict between the orthodox and the Gnostic faiths.

Assembling the Orthodox Canon

Writing in the fourth century, after orthodox

Christianity had followed the example of the heretics and assembled its canon, Eusebius accused the Gnostics of forgery and mutilation of the gospel text (*Ecl. His.*, Book IV, Chap. 22; Book V, Chap 13, 28). The orthodox canon was not in existence when Marcion wrote; neither was it easily assembled afterward. Between the formation of the two canons there was a period of time. How long is not known. Some think a generation or a little over may have elapsed. The orthodox gospels were not collected into one volume such as we know them today. They were scattered in different churches, and it took time and debate to discover their apostolicity and put them into the present form. How many additions or subtractions may have entered into the originals as the two parties tried to make the word conform to the particular ideas of the contenders is difficult to say. All we know is that accusations came from both sides. Which text is the pure one is hard to judge. One evidence, however, appears to be inescapable. Modern scholars have found vast variations and contradictions which, in the minds of some, undermine the physical incarnation of the Lord and distract from the meaning of the gospel. Some of these contradictions, additions, and subtractions will be encountered in this study.

In his book, *The Formation of the New Testament*, Edgar J. Goodspeed makes this observation: "More than one leaf was taken from the book of the thriving sects, and the definitions, organization, and canonization which they had found serviceable were pressed into the service of the general church." He significantly concludes, however, by saying, "If certain vague but precious liberties were sacrificed, some very

21

definite gains were secured."

New Gnostic Material

What added to my belief that the gospels were the issue between the contenders was the discovery of new Gnostic material during this century. Important among them was the discovery in 1930 of Manichaean material in central Asia and also in Egypt. The church may have triumphed over Gnosticism as Eusebius wrote, but a century later Manichaeism came to inflict more damage on the church. The influence of this new Gnosticism according to Hans Jonas extended from the Atlantic in the west to the Indian Ocean in the east. "In the west," he writes, "its missionaries ranged far beyond the areas penetrated by Christianity, and there some branches of the church lasted centuries after its western branches had been suppressed by the victorious Christian Church" (*op. cit.*, p. 207).

Another Gnostic library was discovered in 1946 in Nag Hammadi in Egypt. Due to political influences, not all of it has been translated. Under the auspices of UNESCO an English translation was written by Robert Haardt and published in 1971 by E. J. Brill in Holland. (Unfortunately when it was available to me I was not able to read all of it, but I gathered what I felt was most important.) As a result of this work three more gospels have been added to those already known of the Gnostic gospels; they are the gospel of Truth, the gospel of Thomas, and the gospel of Philip. Hans Jonas apparently was acquainted with this material in German before its translation into English and mentions it in his English book. As I added this to what I had already learned about Gnosticism from previous investigations, I shuddered at the thought of what may happen to the general Christian faith in a day of doubt and excessive cynicism when the information becomes available to the interested public. I have no doubt about the triumph of orthodoxy over Gnosticism, but the scars sustained by the Christian Gospel during the conflict where accusations were made of forgery, mutilation by addition to and subtraction from its text, are plainly to be seen today as students ferret out the contradictions.

Which Gospel?

The new discoveries do not add much to our knowledge of Gnosticism; they simply increase the number of gospels. Gnostic gospels were known to the Christian fathers, and some of them are still in existence today. Not much harm was done by them until the last century when questioning students began the minute examination of the original wording of the Christian Gospel. These heretical gospels were dragged out then and damaging conclusions (faulty though they were) were arrived at. The materialistic atmosphere of the nineteenth century is still with us in the twentieth. This makes the results unavoidably foreseeable.

J. Edgar Bruns, who appears to be in doubt of the orthodox Gospel, may have had this in mind when he wrote:

... The Gnostics have their own good case to make. Basilides, who taught in Egypt around 120, said that he was a disciple of Glaukias, "an interpreter of Peter"; Valentinus, who made a great impact on the Christian scene in Egypt and Rome two decades later, said that he was a disciple of Theodas, a follower of Paul. Scholars do not reject these claims—there is, of course, no way to disprove them—rather, they shrug off the implications by saying that undoubtedly many followers of the apostles misunderstood

23

what they had to say. That is surely true but one must ask: which followers?—J. Edgar Bruns, *The Forbidden Gospel*, Harper and Row, New York, 1976.

The Evidence of Gnostic Abomination

One must bear in mind, however, that when the word "gospel" is used in connection with Gnostic literature, it is misleading. There are no similarities between them and the gospels we know. Christian Gospels deal with objective reality, Christ himself being the sole figure. His teachings, miracles, passion, death, and resurrection are historical facts. Gnostic gospels are different. They are speculative, mythical, and subjective. Anyone attempting to read them will be lost in a world of imagery, symbolism, and theorizing. Their abomination rests in this subjectivity. One example is the bodily resurrection of the Lord mentioned in our orthodox gospels. Here we are dealing with objective reality. He appeared to many of his disciples who saw him with their physical eyes. Men conversed and even ate with him after he vacated the tomb. In my opinion it was the bodily resurrection of Jesus that made the church. Without this resurrection fact it is doubtful that Christianity would have emerged and survived until our day.

When it comes to the resurrection of the body of Jesus, the Gnostics have a different story. They do not even believe that Jesus was crucified. Basilides advanced the idea of substitution. "His passion," he writes, "was a deception, Simon of Cyrene dying on the cross in his shape" (*The Gnostic Religion*, page 133). The Gnostics appear to be consistent in this area. If the flesh is evil, the father of light would not dignify it by death and resurrection.

24

A slightly different account is quoted by Bruns in his *Forbidden Gospel* and comes from the Acts of John. It appears that the suffering of Jesus took place after a dance with his disciples. The men fled, and John hid himself in a nearby cave. Jesus appeared to him and said:

John, in the eyes of the crowd below in Jerusalem I am being crucified and pierced with lances and reeds, and I am being given gall and vinegar to drink, but nothing of the things which they will say of me I have suffered; the suffering which I disclosed to you and to the others in the dance, that I would have called a mystery. What you are you perceive because I showed it to you, but what I am I alone know and no other man.

It is to be noted that the theory of substitution is absent from this account.

Analogous to this is the account of the Koran. In a revelation given to Muhammad at Madina, some 400 to 500 years after Christian Gnosticism had its beginnings, the prophet said:

...and for their unbelief, [the Jews] and their uttering against Mary a mighty calumny, and for their saying, "We slew the Messiah, Jesus son of Mary, the messenger of God"—yet they did not slay him, neither crucified him, only a likeness of that was shown to them. Those who are at variance concerning him surely are in doubt regarding him; they have no knowledge of him, except the following of surmise; and they slew him not of a certainty—no indeed; God raised him up to him; God is All-mighty, All-wise.— Arthur J. Arberry, *The Koran Interpreted*, Oxford University Press.

It appears from this that Gnostic influences, though eradicated in the West, were still alive in the desert. (This reference to the Koran is not to be considered as an indictment against Muhammad or Islam. These subjects require a much greater study than I am able to give here. The quote is used merely to show the widespread influence of Gnosticism.)

I trust that the contribution of this brief review will

become evident as readers discover the confusion in the gospel text and the miraculous manner by which it was corrected in the fullness in advance of modern criticism which exposed the mutilation. I have no hesitancy in saying that Gnosticism is the abomination which has resulted in the removal of the plain and precious truths from the gospel of the Lamb. The early Christian fathers may have been slow in assembling the New Testament canon before the damage was done, but beneath the flimsy cover of contradictions there is a pronounced substratum of the truth of the coming of the Messiah, his teachings, sufferings, crucifixion, and bodily resurrection which served until the period of the great doubt of the nineteenth century. The restoration of the fullness of the gospel is a divine plan, a strategy, devised by the all-knowing Father to meet an emergency in advance of its appearing. It calls for execution by its believers such as the apostolic and patristic missionaries dispensed of their responsibilities.

Here we have *deficiencies* and *fullness*. In our teaching and preaching we have stressed the value of the church, its organization and doctrines, and ignored the deficiencies of the gospel record. Our thanks should go to the critics who discovered these deficiencies for us. Their findings support the prophetic information in the Book of Mormon. But how about the "fullness of the gospel"? No one has validated the truthfulness of this revolutionary statement. Is this angelic declaration of divine origin or was it of human fabrication? The burden of proof rests on those who believe in the Book of Mormon. So far we have been interested in proving the divine origin of the book through archaeological findings. This is good, but no missionary effort has been generated to prove our enthusiastic support of the book. So the problem must lie somewhere else. If I can depend on the study paper prepared for the Department of Christian Education the problem is in the message of the book. Unless the message is validated, the statment of the "fullness of the gospel" remains of human origin.

The Supposed Mistakes in the Book of Mormon

To those who read the Book of Mormon it becomes clear that the book is an abridgment of many records and translations which themselves had been abridged. It is only natural for the last writer to warn us of "faults" in case any appear. He states this in his account which appears in the first page of the book and is again repeated in the book which bears his name. Due to their isolation from their original home and people even the language of this group was changed. In a period of separation which covered nearly a thousand years changes in words and their meaning could take place. But this does not detract from the main theme and purpose of the book—Jesus is the Christ, the eternal God.

In addition to this we have the translation into English. Neither Joseph Smith nor those who acted as scribes were academically prepared for the work which became theirs. As a result mistakes appear in the book, but none of these are substantive. Instead they are mistakes in grammar, spelling, and punctuation. It was the printer, Mr. Grandin, who added the punctuation, corrected some of the grammar, and arranged the paragraphing. In my judgment these mistakes magnify the love of God in the prophetic calling of Joseph Smith. It is the eternal truth in the book, the fullness of the gospel, which counts—not its poor English. "The kingdom of heaven is like unto a treasure hid in the field," said Jesus. It is the treasure we are after in this study. If attention is focused on the grammatical mistakes we shall forever miss the prize. Our New Testament originals were written in poor and not in classical Greek.

Joseph was always aware of his academic deficiency. His scholastic attainments were limited to about a fifth grade education. Oliver Cowdery, his principal scribe, was a schoolteacher but this was of limited help. He and the other two scribes failed to punctuate. There is also evidence of poor spelling. The encounter with the printer must have fired Joseph's determination to improve his education and that of his followers. One of the first undertakings when the group moved from western New York to Kirtland, Ohio, was to erect a temple. A prominent section of the building was assigned to the School of the Prophets.

In the meantime Joseph and Oliver were busy making additional corrections in the manuscript. Fortunately, one of the two manuscripts of the book has been preserved and is in the possession of the Reorganized Church. It is the manuscript that was delivered to Grandin and on which the corrections were made. The authorized edition (the edition used in this study) was carefully compared with previous editions and with the manuscript, and where one or two changes in substance were discovered they were corrected and made to conform with the manuscript. Another edition was issued in 1966. Archaic English was removed, but there was no change in the substance. The preface to both editions explains the motive and change. A photocopy of the manuscript is kept in the church historian's office and can be examined by students. The substantive message of the book is still the same today as it was in 1829.

Joseph's Speculative Theology

There is another reasonable mental block among some people regarding the Book of Mormon. Contributing to this is the speculative theologies of Joseph Smith during the Nauvoo period. Since these theologies are attributed to him personally, some feel that since he was wrong in these speculative teachings he could also be wrong in giving us the Book of Mormon. This, in my judgment, is poor thinking.

What made Joseph Smith a prophet was not his theology of the Nauvoo period but his claim to divine revelation. The revelations he gave are of two kinds: *sensory*, where he claimed that he saw, heard, and touched; and *divine-conceptual*, where he was moved upon by the Holy Spirit. I postulated these in a series of articles which appeared in the *Saints' Herald* September through November of 1968, and the January, February, March, and September issues of 1970. I urge a study of them in conjunction with this work since they were the proposition behind this thesis. On many an occasion as I was writing them I felt that the Reorganization was more Mormon than the group which has taken the name Mormon, because all of our theology is based on the message of the book. We have added nothing.

The Fullness and the Fourth Gospel

Because of the disproportion between the human and the divine, Jesus always shatters our faith before he builds it up. Peter may have spoken the sentiment of the twelve when he said that he would not deny his Lord, but at the sight of Jesus' trial and crucifixion he fled the scene. Even Mary who appeared to remain true to the Lord, when she found the sepulcher empty, said, "they have taken away my Lord." She did not think of his resurrection; she thought of foul play. Her faith was shattered, but with her persistent questioning it returned as she discovered that the One she thought was the gardener was the Lord. As with these early disciples, we have our faith shattered in order that it might be built up. I cannot truthfully say that my faith in the Book of Mormon and the Restoration was not shattered on some occasions, but, like Mary, I continued seeking for an answer. The phrase, "fullness of the gospel," fascinated me as I pursued the problem. The critics helped me find the deficiencies. Could the fullness supply the answer?

The first glimmer of light came when I discovered some thirty-five years ago that the name of John, the apostle of the Lamb, is mentioned in the Book of Mormon. With considerable struggle I took the first step to ascertain the truth or fallacy of the statement. The result was the publication of *Insights into the Book of Revelation*. But that left many a question unanswered. How about Section 7 in the Doctrine and Covenants which deals with the apostle John? And how about the gospel of John which is being battered by the critics? Is it an authentic document written by the apostle? For lack of evidence I made no mention of either in that work. The story is different now. The light continued to be a glimmer until I discovered the unexpected harmony between the fourth gospel and the Book of Mormon account of the Lord's Supper. This is followed by what I believe to be the validation of the gospel of John as an original document written by him as a witness of the ministry, suffering, crucifixion, and resurrection of the Lord. This discovery may not be appreciated by those who are not acquainted with the research which dates the gospel at some time between 150-200 after Christ. The evidence produced by critical students who take this position is strong. Other dedicated researchers shorten this time period considerably, but they still fall short of the traditional goal taken by the early Christian fathers who attributed this gospel to John, the Son of Zebedee. The answer which eluded the students is contained in this study.

The Discovery of Pre-Christian Influence

As believers in the Book of Mormon we accept on faith the story of a miraculous migration from Palestine to America, about 600 years before Christ, of a few individuals of the house of Joseph. Later on another migration took place after the Babylonian captivity. Since the miraculous in the New Testament has been repeatedly under attack, beginning with the times of David Friedrich Strauss, it is to be expected that the miraculous migration story in the Book of Mormon would be doubted. During the period when Joseph Smith told of his angelic experiences there were speculations that the American Indians were descendants of the house of Israel, and most naturally the suspicion arose that Joseph based his theory on the fallacious guessing of the day, making his story sacrosanct by attributing it to heavenly intervention.

31

As one follows the search of leads branching out of the sacrament of the Lord's Supper, however, he will discover what I feel to be unquestionable evidences of teachings and practices in the Book of Mormon not known to the Christian world prior to their disclosure in the book. These can be attributed only to Israelite sources in existence prior to the coming of the Messiah and since lost but recently found. Thus Alexander Campbell's hasty criticism which lumps all the teachings of the Book of Mormon together and attributes them to discussions of the time is proved to be inaccurate.

In chapters five and following of the book of Moroni, readers will find validation for baptism as a symbol of covenant making practiced by the Nephites and also by the Jews long before John the Baptist appeared on the scene. They also will find that circumcision was known only to the Jews, Arabs, ancient Egyptians, and the Aztecs of Central America. They will discover that the inclination for good and evil in man was a divine creation known only to the Jews and the Nephites (as against the dualism of the New Testament). This in itself disposes of the idea of ransom which appears in the New Testament and which bothered Christian theologians for centuries. The word does not appear in connection with the atonement in the Book of Mormon. All of this and more add up to a strong connection between some of the Indians and the people of Palestine long before the advent of the Lord.

"Fullness" and the Resurrection

The Book of Mormon reaches the height of its claim as the fullness of the gospel with its account of the bodily resurrection of Jesus. The resurrection story in the New Testament is lacking considerably in harmony, which often contributes to doubt. If, on the other hand, the story of a migration of Hebrews from Palestine is made credible, then the statement of the Lord concerning the "other sheep" who should hear his voice is clarified. As the tomb was found empty in Jerusalem, the Lord made his presence known to the other sheep of the house of Israel.

Source Material

All my references to the Scriptures are taken from the King James version. Since this work is directed primarily to the members of the Reorganized Church of Jesus Christ of Latter Day Saints, some may wonder why I did not use the Inspired Version. There are four reasons for this: (1) the King James was the only version available to Joseph Smith when the Book of Mormon was written, and to judge a man's work by what he wrote later is not fair; (2) the Inspired Version makes no claim to the fullness of the gospel; (3) this version did not come to the church through angelic ministry; and (4) there are evidences that Joseph was still intending to work on it, even though he wrote that it was completed—otherwise he would have published it during his lifetime. However, I suggest that students use it in comparison of references.

Other source material is referred to at the end of each chapter. Some of this material is readily available in good libraries. Where possible I made references to the *Interpreter's Bible* because of its availability. If the account of the Book of Mormon is to be appraised justly it should be judged by the behavior and religious practices of its own time and not by nineteenth century beliefs. It appeared in that century, but its religious practices date back to centuries before Christ. Literature for this period is hard to find if, indeed, it is ever available in ordinary libraries. The authors whose work I know are listed in the references. I now have a copy of David Friedrich Strauss's work, another of Edershiem's, and the three volumes of George Foot Moore. Emil Schuerer's work is on order and may soon be available. Any student who is willing to pursue the subject may contact me.

As I previously mentioned, this work is intended to cover a special problem in the Reorganization. I would be fortunate, indeed, if it should fall into the hands of students of other faiths and be found of some help. This will be a small fraction of payment for the countless students, Protestants and Catholics, who have devotedly and sacrificially wrestled with the problem trying to maintain the faith. It is their answer to higher criticisms of the Scriptures which has been an inspiration to me. Without their answers I could not have proceeded. I simply built on the foundation they laid.

CHAPTER ONE

HISTORICAL DEVELOPMENT

The word "sacrament" in the Christian sense means something instituted by the Lord. There is evidence that the sacraments have a definite meaning for individuals, and that the observance of them produces certain spiritual benefits. As doubt in the authority of the Scriptures and the divinity of Jesus increases, there is a corresponding erosion in the meaning and efficacy of the sacraments. It would seem that we are living in a period of spiritual uncertainty.

Skepticism enters the life of the individual and society very subtly. Once it begins, however, the results are calamitous. The sacraments were instituted to insulate against this danger. We are told in modern revelation that "in the ordinances. . . the power of godliness is manifest."[1] People in the affluent nations today appear to be floating on a raft of intellectual inflation, constantly fed with material abundance from science and technology. The majority are not aware of the dangers surrounding them. To a few, however, it is becoming quite clear that leaks are beginning to appear, with no permanent remedy in sight. Under such circumstances it becomes the sacred duty of those claiming new revelation from God not only to talk of this revelation and Jesus Christ but to examine the significance of the sacraments in the light of this revelation and the clear need for them. Only such action can bring peace to the human soul.

The central theme of this book is the sacrament of the Lord's Supper. To the majority of Christians it is known as the Eucharist; it will be referred to variously as Mass, Holy Communion, and the Lord's Supper.

Over the years I have observed a beautiful and salutary effect on the lives of those who observe this sacrament in the proper attitude, as contrasted with the lives of those who treat it lightly or ignore it as foolishness. Reasons for questioning the Lord's Supper cannot be gathered under one single heading; however, I believe that a great contributing factor has been the aura of uncertainty which has surrounded the subject. This doubt is probably shared only by theologians and scholars. The average layman is almost totally unaware of it.

The Christian world is divided in its allegiance to this sacrament. The theological history of the Lord's Supper has been one of constant and sometimes violent change. As a people, we are bound to be influenced by this current feeling of uncertainty. In order that we may better understand the changes which have brought this sacrament to its present ambiguous position, we must study the history surrounding its establishment, the development of the doctrine in the primitive church and the metamorphoses which followed, up to the period of higher Bible criticisms. After this we shall study the revealed word on the subject, especially as it came through Joseph Smith, Jr. By making a contrast we shall be able to see this sacrament in the light the Lord has given us.

Instituted by Jesus

A cursory review would indicate that the Lord instituted the sacrament. This is the view held by the fundamentalist. The idea appears in the Synoptic accounts (these three are called the Synoptics because they present a common view) as well as in Paul's writings.[2] When these texts are examined in the light of ensuing history and modern criticism, however, they are found defective. For the primitive church, nevertheless, this sacrament was instituted by Christ himself. Matthew, Mark, and Luke are in perfect agreement that the Lord ate the Passover with his twelve disciples. While Paul omits any mention of a Passover, all four of them agree that as Jesus took bread and wine, he blessed it saying, "This is my body . . . this is my blood." There is a slight difference in Paul's wording regarding the blood. The Synoptics do not contain anything regarding the repetition of the observance. Paul, however, says, "as often as ye eat this bread and drink this cup," indicating repetition. Paul and Luke write that the act is a memorial, while Matthew and Mark are silent on this point. Nevertheless, it is remarkable how much agreement there is among the four writers, especially considering their separation in place and time.

The Lord's Supper in the Apostolic Period

When we leave the upper room where the Lord

ate the Passover meal with his disciples and look for the first observance of it by the company of believers, we become lost. It appears that the earliest Christian community of which we have a record did assemble for a meal.[3] Was the "breaking of bread and prayers" mentioned here the sacrament of the Lord's Supper, or was it the customary Jewish meal observed before the Sabbath had known as the "Kiddush"? The Kiddush was a domestic ceremony observed at home by a family or by a group of friends on the eve of a Sabbath or feast day, in "sanctification" of the event. J. E. Oulton disagrees with this theory on the ground that the Kiddush was a family meal and the mother of Jesus and his brothers were not there.[4] Others who reject the Kiddush theory cling to the possibility that it was the Chaburoth meal. (There are those, however, who disagree with this idea on what seems to them good grounds.)[5] Most likely this meal, the nature of which is still not known to us, was combined with the Lord's Supper. As it was eaten, at some juncture there was a special consecration of bread and wine symbolic of the new covenant the Lord established in his last meal with the Twelve.

Evidence supporting the Chaburoth hypothesis is recorded by Paul in his letter to the Corinthians. Scholars do not completely agree as to the date of the apostle's writing, but there is some evidence that I Corinthians was written some time between A.D. 54 and 55. A joint meal (secular and religious) was still being observed in the Corinthian church at that time, but it had become quite corrupt. This appears to be the burden of Paul's remarks in the

38

tenth and eleventh chapters of I Corinthians. In the opening verses of the tenth chapter he drew a parallel between ancient Israel and the Christian church. The Israelites were baptized in the cloud and in the sea. They also ate and drank of the spiritual food of the Rock that followed them. In spite of all this they perished because of lust, fornication, and idol worship. The sacred and evil cannot be mixed and bring good results. Paul's main point is summed up in the words: "The cup of blessing which we bless, is it not the communion of the blood of Christ?" He concludes by saying, "Ye cannot drink the cup of the Lord, and the cup of devils: ye cannot be partakers of the Lord's table, and the table of devils."

Lust, fornication, and idol worship were not the only vices of the Corinthians. They were also guilty of heresies, gluttony, and drunkenness in their church meals. This is the burden of a portion of the last half of the eleventh chapter:

> When ye come together therefore into one place, this is not to eat the Lord's supper. For in eating every one taketh before other his own supper: and one is hungry, and another is drunken. What? have ye not houses to eat and to drink in? or despise ye the church of God, and shame them that have not?...I praise you not.[6]

After this reprimand Paul went on to explain that he received from the Lord instructions regarding the Communion and how it should be observed.[7]

Obvious conclusions can be drawn from Paul's instructions to the Corinthians. As late as the writing of his first letter to them the Lord's Supper was observed in connection with a meal the nature of which is not definitely known. Was Paul attempting to separate this meal from the Lord's Supper? Did he succeed? No one can answer with certainty. The *Didache*, a Christian manual of discipline written during the second century, gives instructions regarding the Eucharist. Apparently the joint meal of supper and the Eucharist was still being observed at that time. The manual states after that the participant is "satisfied with food" a Eucharist prayer was made.[8] Separation of the Lord's Supper from a meal, on the nature of which there is lack of agreement, came gradually.

Meaning of the Lord's Supper

Not long after the appearance of Paul's letter to the Corinthians came the Gospel According to Mark, followed by Matthew and Luke. No one can be certain of the exact dates of these gospels. Some think that Mark appeared in the sixties and, after some interval, Matthew and Luke in the seventies. The important thing for us is the unity they present on their accounts of the Lord's Supper. These gospels all connect the last meal with the Jewish Passover. The three books are also very similar in their wording of the institution of the sacrament and Paul agrees with them on this. Out of the similarities among these writers developed the meaning of this sacrament.

The first significant meaning to gain acceptance was the "covenant" idea. The Synoptic writers as well as Paul use the words "new testament."[9] This is a very important observation. If the Lord's Supper was the new Passover and was observed on that day in the Jewish calendar, then the idea of the covenant follows naturally. After the Israelites were delivered from Egyptian bondage, they traveled to Mount Sinai where the Lord made his covenant with them.[10] Israel, however, did not live up to the terms of the covenant. For this reason Jeremiah prophesied of a time to come when the Lord would make a new covenant with the people.[11] Jesus fulfilled this prophecy in the memorable supper with the Twelve.

The second significant meaning to gain acceptance was that of sacrifice. The paschal lamb had to be one without blemish, and after it was killed its blood was to be painted on both sides and the top of the door.[12] Its meat was to be roasted and eaten with unleavened bread, indicating the speed with which the Israelites were to leave Egypt on their journey to the promised land. The church looked at Christ as the paschal lamb sacrificed for the sins of man. He became the Lamb of the new covenant. John, who seems to disagree with the Passover theory, mentions the fact that none of Christ's bones were broken, indicating that the Lord was sinless.[13] Similarly, in Revelation he is referred to as "a Lamb as it had been slain."[14] For this reason he is referred to as the "Redeemer" and "Savior."

One might add a subheading dealing with the corporality of the bread and wine. The statement, "This is my body," is found in the Synoptic as well as Pauline instructions. The statement was interpreted literally in the primitive church, and as late as A.D. 150 Justin Martyr associated the bread and wine with the body of the Lord. He wrote:

> For not as common bread and common drink do we receive these; but in like manner as Jesus Christ our Savior, having

been made flesh by the word of God, has both flesh and blood for our salvation, so likewise have we been taught that the food which is blessed by the power of his word, and from which our flesh and blood by transmutation are nourished, is the flesh and blood of that Jesus who was made flesh.[15]

Most authorities agree that John's was the last of the gospels to appear. The sixth chapter repeats in different phraseology from the Synoptics and Paul that the flesh of Christ is "meat indeed" and his blood is "drink indeed." John goes on to report: "He that eateth my flesh, and drinketh my blood, dwelleth in me and I in him."[16] These statements supported the Synoptic claims and gave the church added evidence of the corporal presence of Christ in the Eucharist. This literal interpretation was to plunge the church into endless debate and deep schism.

Of singular interest here is the fact that, during most of the first two centuries, there is no evidence of either a theological or philosophical attempt to justify this explanation of the bread and wine as the actual body of Christ. The idea was accepted on faith. It was not until the last part of the second century and the first part of the third that a rational explanation was made. Tertullian, Cyprian, and Saint Augustine stressed the symbolic significance of the bread and wine, but their ideas did not take hold of the mentality of the day.

The Conversion Theory

This theory stresses the actual presence of Christ in the bread and wine and attempts to explain the change. Its advocate was Cyril, Bishop of Jerusalem.[17] The subject of the Trinity was an issue at the time, and the Holy Spirit was emphasized by some part of the Godhead. Proponents of the conversion theory postulated that when the Eucharistic prayers were uttered over the bread and wine, the emblems became the actual flesh and blood of Jesus. Gregory of Nyssa carried the idea a bit further. The objects were "trans-made" or "transclemented." According to Gregory, just as food taken by the mouth and digested in the stomach becomes metabolized into the flesh and blood of the individual, so was the bread and wine metabolized in the life of the participant. By A.D. 759, with the appearance of John of Damascus, the conversion theory was an established fact in the Greek churches of the East.[18]

The story was different in the West. The conversion theory was introduced there by Ambrose of Milan in A.D. 397, but the West was still under the influence of the symbolic interpretation taught by Augustine. The sacrament was to be regarded as divine; in it "one thing is seen, but another is understood."[19] The bread and wine were sanctified so that they became the sacrament. As such they communicated a supernatural gift, but they themselves were not the gift. Although the Augustinian theory held firmly, it was not without challengers. Some supporters of Ambrose wrote extensively on the subject. These writings did not fire the imagination of the time, but by the middle of the ninth century they came back to light, and a prolonged and acrimonious debate followed.

In the thirteenth century the balance tipped in favor of the conversion thesis. The term which was used in the West for this transformation was "transubstantiation" as opposed to the East's "transelemented."

Thomas Aquinas refined the doctrine and made it philosophically acceptable, and Roman Catholics hold this view of the Lord's Supper today. The symbolism of Augustine was not completely dead, however. It would rise again in the Reformation.

The Sacrifice Theory

Simultaneously with these developments other side issues became associated with the sacrament. Since the Lord's Supper was the new Passover, and since it was the actual body of Christ which was being sacrificed, it was inevitable that a priest should offer the sacrifice. As early as A.D. 108, Ignatius of Antioch insisted that if the Eucharist was to be genuine, a bishop or one appointed by him should perform it. The early Christians were accused by the pagans of being atheists because they had no sacrifice and no temple. In order to meet this accusation the Christians supposedly developed the sacrifice of the Mass with specially ordained priesthood.[20] Simultaneously with this development of priestly authority came confession, absolution, and the denial of the wine to the laity.

The Lord's Supper and the Reformation

With the coming of the Reformation, a new chapter was added to the already confusing claims of the established church of the time. Martin Luther was a priest in the Roman church, and as he turned his back on special priesthood and insisted on the priesthood of all believers, it was natural that his views on the Lord's Supper would undergo change. He believed not in *transubstantiation* but *consubstantia-*

tion,[21] which means that the substance of the bread and wine remain as they are and become associated in the mind of the participant with the substance of the Lord. Luther's insistence on consubstantiation generated heated debate. He also held the view that the wine was not for the priest only but that the laity should also receive it as they received the bread. According to Luther, the Lord's Supper could not be sacrificed by a priest, since Christ was the only priest.

The Swiss theologian Zwingli took a different stand. He regarded the statement, "This is my body" as a sign (symbol), and by so doing he lined up with the Augustinian thesis. Luther and Zwingli debated this stand with no appreciable results, and Zwingli was accused of being negative.[22]

When Calvin entered the picture he assumed the role of mediator. The elements were not only signs such as Zwingli advocated but also instruments of grace. This made a big difference. When the believer partook of the emblems, he was not taking the substance of the Lord's body with the bread but was partaking of the saving power of the body of Christ.[23]

With the advent of rationalism it was inevitable that the claims of these reformers would be challenged. The idea of the miraculous and the impartation of grace does not appeal to a scientifically and intellectually oriented community. Some of the rationalists followed the Quakers in rejecting all outward sacramental observances, clinging to the inward and spiritual. They could not see how a man could transform the bread and wine into the substance of the body of Christ by saying "Hoc est corpus meum." From that statement grew the slang expression "hocus pocus."

But the majority of Protestants were united on the commemorative aspect of the Lord's Supper. The words from Paul and Luke, "this do in remembrance of me," rose in value for the first time.

What we have seen thus far is simply the struggle of men to affirm their faith. As we enter into a new phase of the study of the Lord's Supper—a phase noted for its negation rather than for its affirmation—a background such as this will become helpful.

1. Doctrine and Covenants 83:3c.
2. Matthew 26:17-30; Mark 14:12-26; Luke 22:7-20; I Corinthians 11:23-26.
3. Acts 2:41 ff
4. J. E. Oulton, *Holy Communion and Holy Spirit*, London, S.P.C.K., 1954.
5. For the argument pro and con one should read *The Lord's Supper* by William Barclay, SCM Press Ltd., London, 1967, pp. 30-31.
6. I Corinthians 11:20-22.
7. I Corinthians 11:23 ff.
8. 10:1 Krisopp Lake Translation.
9. Matthew 26:14-16; Mark 14:24; Luke 22:20; I Corinthians 11:25.
10. Exodus 19-24.
11. Jeremiah 31:31-33.
12. Exodus 12:7.
13. John 19:36.
14. Revelation 5:6.
15. *Justin Martyr's First Apology*, Chapter 66, Antenicene Christian Library, Edinburgh.
16. John 6:56.
17. William Barclay, *The Lord's Supper*, *op. cit.*, p. 65.
18. *Ibid.*, pp. 67-68.
19. *Ibid.*, p. 69.
20. *Ibid.*, pp. 81-83.
21. Williston Walker, *A History of the Christian Church*, Charles Scribner's Sons, New York, 1925, p. 345.
22. *Ibid.*, pp. 363-364.
23. *Ibid.*, p. 394.

CHAPTER TWO

THE CRITICAL INVESTIGATION

The early Christian fathers and those who followed them in the Orthodox, Catholic, and Protestant faiths depended on the authority of the inspired word as they studied the Lord's Supper. The period of "higher criticism" presented a different problem, for during this era the authenticity of the word itself was questioned. The influence of this period has brought Catholic and Protestant theological views closer together than at any post-Reformation time. It is here that liberalism (as against fundamentalism) was born. The general belief of the laity, on the other hand, has been undergoing erosion. Perhaps the layman is tired of theological hairsplitting at a time of excessive rationalism.

As we study critical works on the Lord's Supper, we will discover that the conclusions of former theologians were completely invalidated. Where they were sure that the Lord instituted the sacrament of the Communion, theological critics ask, "Did he?" Where former scholars affirmed that the Lord ate the Passover meal with his disciples, present scholars ask, "How could he have done it?" And where earlier researchers rested their case by depending on the divine authority of the New Testament account, those of today see a contradictory meaning behind that account.

The Passover

For almost 1,800 years the Christian church believed that the Lord and his apostles literally observed the Jewish Passover. The authority of the Synoptic writers and Paul was unquestioned. Matthew wrote: "Now the first day of the feast of unleavened bread the disciples came to Jesus, saying unto him, Where wilt thou that we prepare for thee to eat the passover?" The Lord directed them to go to a man in a certain town and tell him, "I will keep the passover at thy house with my disciples."[1]

The same incident was recorded by Mark with a very slight variation. The disciples asked Jesus, "Where wilt thou that we go and prepare that thou mayest eat the passover?"[2] They followed his directions "and made ready the passover."[3] The story was also recorded by Luke but with a significant variation. In the first two cases the disciples took the initiative. Luke, on the other hand, said that Jesus initiated the idea of preparing for the Passover: "He sent Peter and John saying, Go and prepare us the passover, that we may eat." Luke attributes another statement to the Lord which is not found in the other accounts. Jesus said: ". . . With desire I have desired to eat this passover with you before I suffer."[4] Aside from initiating the thought of celebrating the Passover, he was anxious to observe it with them at this important time because this Passover was to be different from all previous ones.

In order to understand what the critic is saying, it

will be helpful to learn how the Passover was instituted in ancient Israel and how it was to be observed.[5]

1. It was to begin on the fourteenth day of the first month, Nisan. (The Jewish day began with sunset and ended at sunset the following day.)

2. A yearling male lamb, without blemish was to be set apart for sacrifice. Its blood was to be painted on both sides of the door as well as on the top post. The lamb was to be roasted and eaten that night, and none of those participating were to leave the house until morning.

3. For seven days they were to eat nothing but unleavened bread.

4. This day was to be observed as a memorial throughout the generations of Israel. Even when they came to the land of promise, the day was to be observed.

5. When children asked about this strange meal and behavior, their father was to recite to them the story of Egyptian slavery; how the Lord delivered them from bondage; how the Egyptian firstborn males died while they were spared; and how the Lord brought them to the land flowing with milk and honey.

6. It was to be observed "at the place which the Lord thy God shall choose"[6] which at the time of Jesus was Jerusalem.

In addition, through the years Jewish traditions were developed which, by the time of the Lord, had become part of the Passover worship. Four cups of wine were to be taken at intervals, reminding the participant of the four promises of God to the nation.[7] Also there was the recitation of the Hallel (Psalms 113-118), songs of praise and thanksgiving. The cups of wine were drunk and the psalms were sung alternately. There were also bitter herbs for the meal, indicating the bitterness of their bondage in Egypt.[8]

When critics compare the observance of the Lord's Supper as recorded in the New Testament with the rules of observance as given in the law and practiced by the Jews, they find bewildering inconsistencies.

The Synoptic writers agree that the Lord ate the Passover meal with his disciples. The critic, on the other hand, finds this unacceptable. This year the fourteenth of Nisan fell at sunset Friday and ended with sunset Saturday. This is the Passover day. The lamb is slain in the temple Friday noon, the day of preparation. The Passover meal starts at sunset the same day (beginning Saturday) and lasts until midnight. According to this account the trial and crucifixion of Jesus took place on Saturday. This would place the resurrection some time on Monday instead of the first day of the week. In addition to this the Lord was a good Jew and so were his disciples. In comparing the observance as recorded by the Synoptics with the Jewish observance we find several violations:

1. After eating the Passover, why should the Lord and the disciples leave the house and go to the Garden of Gethsemane when it was not lawful to leave the house where the meal was eaten until morning?
2. A flurry of activities started at Gethsemane and continued until the Lord is sentenced:
   a. Judas went and bargained with the high priests on the price he was to get for delivering Jesus to them.[9]

b. A "multitude" of Jews came to arrest Jesus.

c. One of those with Jesus drew his sword and committed a violent act.

d. After this Jesus was taken to the house of the high priest for trial.

e. As the sun came up, "the elders of the people and the chief priests and the scribes came together, and led him into their council," and the trial began.[10]

f. After the Jews were through questioning Jesus, they took him to Pilate, preferred charges, and asked for the death penalty.

All this happened during the first day of the Passover feast, from sunset Friday evening to sunrise Saturday morning. How could these Jews and their spiritual leaders desecrate the Passover? Some critics say this could not have happened on the most sacred of the Jewish holy days, and it is therefore obvious that the Lord did not eat the Passover.[11]

The problem is made doubly acute when the gospel according to John is found to disagree with the Synoptics on this subject. The author of John, the critic argues, was apparently acquainted with the Christian records which preceded his account. Was John trying to correct their errors? Some think so. John did not write on the subject of the Lord's Supper as such, but his writings alluded to it. Nowhere did he mention the Passover meal as being the Lord's Supper. But he said, "Now before the feast of the passover, . . ." Jesus had a meal with his disciples. "And supper being ended, the devil having now put into the heart of Judas Iscariot, Simon's son, to betray him . . ."[12] Though the meal is not referred to as the Lord's Supper, its connection with

Judas' betrayal leads scholars to this conclusion.

Most of the critics now agree with the account of John—that Jesus ate a meal before the Passover. John also appears to be consistent in that the arrest and trial of Jesus took place the day before the Passover—the day of preparation. It started Thursday evening at six o'clock, the time that Jesus ate the meal with his disciples. In that case Jesus and his disciples would not have violated the Passover rules by eating and going out that same night to Gethsemane. Neither would Judas have violated the observance of the Passover by transacting business with the high priest. The same would have applied to the "multitude" which arrested Jesus, the trial before the high priest, and the final stand before Pilate. In all of these activities John was consistent. He made it completely clear that all of these transactions happened on the day of preparation.[13] Also, this same consistency was revealed when he wrote: "Then led they Jesus from Caiaphas unto the hall of judgment; and it was early; and they themselves went not into the judgment hall, lest they should be defiled; but that they might eat the passover."[14] It may be noted that the phrase "it was early" in this verse agrees with Luke's observation that "as soon as it was day" they took Jesus for trial.[15] The only difference was in the day. It was on the thirteenth, not on the fourteenth of Nisan. This account places the resurrection on Sunday instead of Monday.

One can easily imagine what the conflict between the Synoptic accounts and that of John has done to ancient and deeply entrenched beliefs. The greatest damage has been experienced by the Roman Catholics and the Eastern churches. When the Lord's Supper was regarded as the ancient Passover of the Jews, its observance required sacrifices performed by the priesthood. The whole worship experience centered around the mass. Now, since scholars believe John implied that the Lord did not eat the Passover, Roman Catholic and Eastern theology has suffered a great setback. There has been a studious and disciplined attempt among theologians of these faiths to find a way out of this dilemma. A French scholar, Jean Danielou, advanced a new theory as he discussed the theological implications of the discovery of the Dead Sea Scrolls. According to him there were two different calendars among the Jews. The people of the community of Qumran had a calendar which differed from the Jewish calendar by one day. This means that when the Jews were celebrating the Passover on the fourteenth of Nisan, the Qumran people were celebrating it a day earlier. Danielou wrote:

> The problem would be solved if it could be shown that at that time there were two different dates for the celebration of Passover. Now there exists an old tradition according to which Christ is supposed to have partaken of the Passover meal on Tuesday evening, and to have been arrested on Wednesday and crucified on Friday. This tradition has been neglected up to now. Mlle. Jubert has shown that the people of Qumran used an old priestly calendar of 364 days, containing four trimesters of 91 days, each of which had 13 weeks. Since there were exactly 52 weeks in the year, feast days, according to this calendar, necessarily fell on the same day of the month and of the week. Furthermore, in this calendar Passover always fell on Wednesday.[16]

This contribution is most interesting. Scholars have suspected a calendar different from the one in current use. If this is sustained by further investigation, there will emerge a completely different attitude toward this important sacrament. So far none has emerged.

Going back to the Synoptics, we find that the issue of the Passover meal is further clouded by the omission of any mention of the Passover lamb, which was the basic feature of the Passover observance. Also unleavened bread is not mentioned at all; it appears that ordinary leavened bread was being used. Finally, the four cups which were part of the Passover tradition among the Jews of the day are not mentioned.[17]

Paul Instituted the Lord's Supper

Because of the wide disagreement between the Synoptic accounts and that of John, and because of the similarities between Paul's and Luke's accounts regarding the wording of the institution, a number of critics attribute the origin of the Lord's Supper to Paul rather than to Jesus. Their reasoning is based on two different statements by Paul. The first is "this do in remembrance of me."[18] These exact words appear in Luke.[19] The verse following reads "This cup is the new testament in my blood."[20] The same words are found in Luke.[21] The only difference is in the instructions to repeat the observance. If we were to write Luke's and Paul's descriptions of the institution next to each other, we would find definite exactitude. This has led scholars to assume that, since Luke was a companion to Paul on some of his missionary travels, Luke copied his formula for the institution from Paul.

Another observation supporting the authorship of Paul is his claim to a special revelatory experience from Christ in which he was told what to say and do. In the opening statement of his instructions regarding the Lord's Supper, he says: "For I have received of the Lord that which also I delivered to you."[22] How did Paul "receive of the Lord" when he was not with the Twelve the night of the Last Supper? The obvious answer is that he received by revelation. This is the way by which he came to acknowledge Christ—his visionary experience while on the way to Damascus. Few critics argue that Paul was susceptible to mystical experiences in which he saw and heard things which he attributed to God. Had Christ instituted the Lord's Supper, the Synoptic writers would not have made the mistake of saying it was the Passover.

In support of Paul's authorship, critics refer to the mystery religions. Almost all of these had a rite similar to the Lord's Supper, and the critics claim that Paul, during his contact with these religions, became impressed with this rite and brought it to the Christian Church. In support of this theory, they refer to Justin Martyr's vivid description of this sacrament as it was observed in his day. Knowing of the similarity between it and the mystic rite in Mithraism, he wrote: "Which the devils have imitated in the mysteries of Mithra, commanding the same thing be done."[23] The question is, who imitated whom? And the answer becomes obvious. Mithraism is older than Christianity, so it must be that the younger imitated the older.

The Missing Prayer

Another issue is the apparent loss of the prayer which the Lord taught his disciples to pray over the bread and wine. There is no mention of this in the New Testament, but Justin Martyr—who wrote around A.D. 150—refers to it. This early date is significant to a study of the Lord's Supper. Sometime between A.D. 100 and 150, as far as critical research reveals, the Gospel According to John appeared, and Justin's *Apology* followed soon after. This early date gives Justin's statement a strong note of authority, especially when the investigation of the origin and meaning of the Lord's Supper has given rise to so much concern.

First, we should consider Justin's complete statement so we can be in a better position to understand both sides of the subject. He wrote:

> And this food is called among us the Eucharist, of which no one is allowed to partake but the man who believes that the things which we teach are true, and who has been washed with the washing that is for the remission of sins, and unto regeneration, and who is living as Christ has enjoined. For not as common bread and common drink do we receive these; but in like manner as Jesus Christ our Saviour, having been made flesh by the word of God, had both flesh and blood for our salvation, so likewise have we been taught that the food *which is blessed by the prayer of His Word* [italics mine] and from which our flesh and blood by transmutation are nourished, is the flesh and blood of that Jesus who was made flesh. For the apostles in the memoirs composed by them, which are called Gospels, have thus delivered unto us what was enjoined upon them; that Jesus took bread, and when He had given thanks, He said, This do in remembrance of me, this is my body, and that after the same manner, having taken the cup and giving thanks, he said, This is my blood; and gave it to them alone, which the wicked devils have imitated in the mysteries of Mithra, commanding the same thing to be done.[24]

The phrase, "by the prayer of His Word," may seem confusing. However, students agree that it refers to the prayer the Lord taught his disciples to pray over the bread and wine. Gildersleeve, who translated Justin Martyr's First Apology, wrote: "His Word is commonly understood as the prayer of blessing pronounced by Christ at the time of instituting the Eucharist."[25]

In order to meet the objections of the critics, proponents of the conversion theory appealed to Justin's First Apology. The argument was that the Lord taught the disciples a prayer which, when repeated over the emblems, naturally changed their substance. This argument did not daunt the critics, however. They argued that, if Christ taught his disciples such a prayer, no one knew what the prayer was because it was not found anywhere in ancient literature.

This problem was temporarily solved by the discovery of the *Teachings of the Apostles*, an ancient text which was mentioned in the writings of the early Christian fathers but could not be found at the time. This small Christian manual, commonly known as *The Didache*, was discovered in 1873 in a church library in Constantinople. There is considerable debate as to its date of origin, although there is general agreement that some of its material dates from the period between A.D. 90 and 120. Most scholars believe that it was not authored by one man.

There are three sections in the *Didache* which deal with instructions about the Lord's Supper, and scholars during the latter 1800s thought that one of the prayers mentioned was the prayer the Lord pronounced on the bread and wine. At that time, however, the discovery was still fresh and enthusiasm was not yet tempered by sound judgment. Modern students reject this assumption because the prayer does not mention the emblems, and the consensus is that this is a prayer of benediction. The prayer is, therefore, still lost to the world.

Believers conclude that it makes no difference what words one may say over the emblems as long as a prayer of blessing is uttered. To the critic, on the other hand, the loss of this prayer is another cause for doubt. The late Bishop Gore treats the believer's viewpoint in detail in his *Body of the Christ*.[26] Bishop E. W. Barnes presents the critic's stand in his *The Rise of Christianity*.[27]

In support of his orthodox claims about the authenticity of the Lord's Supper, Dr. Gore quotes Justin Martyr's First Apology. However, when it comes to explaining the absence of the prayer on the emblems that the Lord taught his disciples, he becomes evasive:

What exactly Justin Martyr means by the prayer word which is from Christ, by which the Eucharist is blessed, is, and will probably remain, uncertain. Any form of benediction of the elements believed by the church to be substantially those used by Christ, or any form of prayer repeating His words of institution, would answer sufficiently to Justin's description. The suggestion that Justin means the Lord's Prayer is surely improbable. The Lord's prayer is not a form of thanksgiving or benediction over food.[28]

Barnes, on the other hand, appears to dismiss lightly the importance of "the prayer word which comes from Him." He writes: "From the account which Justin gives there appears to have been no set form of consecration prayer."[29] The difficulty here is in the translation of Justin's Apology. Its source is Greek. Gore's translation reads: "By the word of prayer which comes from Him" while Barnes' translation reads: "By the prayer of the Logos [word] which comes from Him."[30]

Because of the importance of this missing prayer to our future study, both of the preceding translations have been quoted. The impartial interpretation, however, seems to favor Gore's translation.

Bishop Barnes's highly improbable conclusions go much further than his singular interpretation of Justin's Apology. He doubts that Jesus ever instituted the Lord's Supper and attributes its origin to the imitation of the mystery religions of the day. "In the earliest Christian period," he writes, "the Eucharist, whatever its origin or initial form, was associated with a complete meal, as we realize from the first epistle to the Corinthians. But the fact that, alike in this epistle and in all the three Synoptic gospels, substantially the same story of its origin was told, was deemed proof positive that it was based upon the action and command of Jesus. This belief . . . can no longer be easily held."[31]

In chapter sixteen Barnes presents scholarly opinions which attack the validity of the New Testament account of the subject.

In the first place, a majority of independent scholars are of the opinion that at the Last Supper Jesus did not say, "Do this in remembrance of me." Secondly, a minority of such scholars, which seems to be steadily growing, would add that the sentences, "This is my body," "this is my blood," are equally unhistorical. Scholars in this minority contend that the story, as we have it in slightly different form in the First Epistle to the Corinthians, in the Synoptic Gospels, and in the first Apology of Justin Martyr, grew up as an attempt to give Christ's authority to the existing cult practice of the common meal.[32]

In discussing Luke's account of the Lord's Supper, Barnes says:

We must not expect to find decisive evidence . . . to the Lukan story. From these books all sharp contradictions, if they existed, have been removed. The books were, for the most part, made authoritative in the second century of our era; and we must assume that they were then edited so as to remove harsh discrepancies. If a book could not be so edited it was discarded. For this reason the *Didache* was set aside.

Barnes concludes that the story of the Lord's Supper as written by Luke "owes its form to the influence of the mystery-faiths, in which, . . . mystical preparation in the death of the saviour-God leads to a share in his immortality."[33]

The Problem of the Original Text

I have thus far discussed a number of problems which

have faced students dealing with the origin and meaning of the Lord's Supper. On purpose I have left the thorniest of these for last—the problem of the different texts. The Lord wrote no book regarding his mission and teachings, and neither did those disciples who were closest to him. They were living in the expectancy of his immediate return. The four Gospels as we have them date to the fourth century. In the interim, Christ's sayings were preserved by tradition and in time were written and canonized. This canonization was not arrived at peacefully. The period was characterized by philosophical and theological tension which was bitter and divisive. As the strife of the contending parties increased, a resort to apostolic authority was inevitable. Deletions from and additions to the sayings and story of Jesus were multiplied in this contentious atmosphere.[34]

Whatever was written at the beginning of the conflicts was written by hand, perhaps on papyrus, and thus could survive only in the dry climate of Egypt. What was written was also intended to be read to the public since not all the people could read. As copies were made of the original, the copyist was naturally influenced by his own philosophical and doctrinal leanings. He could insert or subtract words—an action he would consider simply as "correcting." What he had heard also became a prime factor as he wrote. As time passed and more copies were made, more additions were inserted to conform with accepted tradition of the area. The King James Version is an example of this blending.

Since the middle of the last century, as interest in higher criticism has become universal among Christians, thousands of fragments of manuscript have been discovered and studied. The variations among them have increased in number. Students also have discovered what Ernest C. Colwell calls "cross-breeding." He concludes his article with, "Since the discovery of hitherto unknown materials proceeds apace, all such lists are out of date within five years of publication. Only the specialist can be expected to keep abreast of this flood." In the opening paragraphs he makes this observation: ". . . the original documents are gone—sunk without a trace in the vast and misty sea of the past. . . . The originals of each book of the New Testament have vanished."[35]

What have not vanished, however, are the second and third generations of the original family of manuscripts. Unfortunately we know nothing about the original; we know only that there are resemblances among the descendants. Nevertheless, the variations have become much greater than the resemblances as time has gone by. This is true of the many texts and families of texts which make up our modern New Testament.

An example of this differentiation is given in the article by Sherman E. Johnson in his introduction to the *Gospel According to St. Matthew*; Section X is the most interesting one. He writes:

> The King James Version was made from a type of Greek text, usually known as the Byzantine, Koine, or K text, which grew up from the fourth century on. One of the characteristics of this text—also found in other text types—is its fullness. If, in a given verse, two or more earlier groups of manuscripts had more than one reading, the tendency of later scribes was to combine them into a longer reading.

He compares four texts, and the "K text in the great majority of cases represented the poorer reading."[36]

It was this variation in the wording of the different

texts regarding the Lord's Supper and the manuscripts which came from them that caused Barclay to write:

> The identification of the words of its institution presents a tangled, and perhaps even an unsoluble, problem. This problem would remain for even the most determined fundamentalist, who insists on taking the words of the scripture exactly as they stand, for he as much as any one else, would have to decide which version of the words as they stand he proposed to take.[37]

In support of his contention, Barclay cites controversial Luke with his longer and shorter texts. He compares the longer text with four other shorter ones. Two of the shorter texts—the "D in some Latin Mss" and "the Curetonian Syriac"—omit the "New Covenant" and "to the remembering of me." Of special interest here is the fact that as need arose for up-to-date versions of the New Testament, both the Revised Standard and the New English Bible used the shorter text. The exact translations are here quoted. First, from the Revised Standard Version, 22:17-22:

> And he took a cup, and when he had given thanks he said; "Take this, and divide it among yourselves; [18]for I tell you that from now on I shall not drink of the fruit of the vine until the kingdom of God comes." [19]And he took bread, and when he had given thanks he broke it and gave it to them, saying, "This is my body. [21]But behold the hand of him who betrays me is with me on the table."

There is no twentieth verse in this version, and neither the covenant nor the remembrance are mentioned.

The New English Version does not divide the language into verses, but the substance is the same:

> Then he took a cup, and after giving thanks he said, 'Take this and share it among yourselves; for I tell you, from this moment I shall drink from the fruit of the vine no more until the kingdom of God comes.' And he took bread, gave thanks, and broke it; and he gave it to them, with the words: 'This is my body.'

A comparison of these verses with those of the King James Version would show the variation and the immensity of the problem. All come from ancient texts. The same is also true of Mark 14:24. The King James Version uses the term "New Testament." The Revised Standard Version and the New English Version omit the word "New." Exactly the same change appears in Matthew 26-28—the word "new" is absent.

The translators of these versions are honest in that they list in a footnote how "other ancient authorities" make the verse read. In so doing they leave the reader to make the choice.

The question naturally arises: How did these men make the transition and arrive at the preceding decisions? The reasoning behind it is this: Since there are now so many texts and since these texts have been influenced by tradition and intermixing, the shorter text is more likely to have fewer additions and thus be nearer to what the Lord said. If additional earlier texts should be found, more changes will undoubtedly take place.

The Bewildering Implication

Out of this critical review regarding the Lord's Supper some faith-shaking implications emerge, the repercussions of which are already being felt. Christianity is facing a major crisis, and so is the Reorganized Church. The Lord's Supper is only one phase of the problem. Central to this crisis is the authority of the New Testament. The Old and New Testaments were the authority to the Christian Church. Christ always referred to the prophets and the Old Testament as the source of authority, and so did the early writers of the New Testament when arguing with the Jews. The Scriptures to them were inspired by God.[38] Now we are finding that there were man-made changes, thus confusing the account. We do not know what is of God and what is of man. To the critics the Scriptures are therefore errant.

The theological arguments of the Reformation were based on a common acceptance of the Scriptures as the word of God. Luther based his protest against the Catholic Church on the inerrant Word. As the debate between Luther, Zwingli, and Calvin intensified, the contending parties each resorted to the New Testament in support of his particular position. With the discovery of the printing press and the increase in literacy, interpretations of the Word of God multiplied. Different men interpreted the word differently. This in turn gave rise to denominationalism.

With the discovery that the Bible is fallible, however, denominational walls have been in the process of tumbling. Theologians of late insist on minimizing the name of the sect and putting the emphasis on "Christian." As a result of this new emphasis, the education of the member is undergoing change. Prior to the discovery that the Scriptures were errant, the education of the individual was grounded in the sectarian beliefs. Now, however, the focus is on "Christian education," which is directed toward unifying the "body of Christ."

William Barclay gives the strong impression of holding this viewpoint in his book. He is honest in detailing the complex problem facing theologians and puts it in understandable terms for the layman. In effect he is saying that we should cease our divisions and arguments. These differences have come to us from a past when our Christian forefathers believed that the Scriptures were written by the hand of God. Now we are finding things to be different. The hand of man entered in and made some major changes in the recorded word, and we are unable to recapture the details. The only sure thing we know is that the purpose of the Lord's Supper is to establish "unity" among the believers and to recall the "memory" of Jesus.[39]

We find further evidence of this trend in a book recently written by a Roman Catholic priest, Ernest J. Fiedler, and a Methodist minister, R. Benjamin Garrison.[40] They are honest in approaching their task of divorcing themselves from their sectarian beliefs and devoting their efforts toward ecumenicity. It is interesting to note Garrison's reasoning in favor of infant baptism and Fiedler's justification for divorcing himself from the theology of the Council of Trent. For the sake of brevity, only the latter will be quoted:

Regarding the specific question of Trent and the concept of sacrifice. . .I repeat and would like to do so with considerable emphasis, these were theologians plying their trade; theologizing. . . .However, such ideas represent individual opinion or, at most, a school of thought, not an official, settled, doctrinal consensus or position of a church.[41]

Of supreme interest to us is Garrison's quote from *Unity Trends* showing how the theological antagonists of four centuries ago—Roman Catholics and Lutherans—are today settling the problem of division and approaching unity. This is their joint statement:

The Catholic affirmation that the church offers Christ in the mass has in the course of the last half century been increasingly explained in terms which answer Lutheran fears that this detracts from the full sufficiency of Christ's sacrifice. . . .Apart from Christ we have no gift, no worship, no sacrifice of our own to offer to God.[42]

Recently the news media carried the announcement that agreement had been reached between Roman

Catholic bishops and those of the Anglican Church (Episcopalians) on the sacrament of the Lord's Supper. So the drift toward ecumenicity is gaining momentum, although the word "ecumenical" is being minimized of late.

Fundamentalism and the Lord's Supper

Fundamentalism, on the other hand, takes a completely different stance. From its inception, this movement had been consistent. It gained prominence in North America (in Dayton, Tennessee) when John Scopes was tried and convicted on the issue of teaching evolution. As in that case it stood for the inerrancy of the Scriptures, it does so now regarding the belief and practice of the Lord's Supper.

The fundamentalist is well acquainted with biblical criticism concerning the origin of the Lord's Supper. In answer to the critic he refers to the primitive church and the tradition established there. A recent fundamentalist spokesman on the Lord's Supper, G. C. Berkouwer, admits that

the decision here will always depend upon the significance that one ascribes to the authority of Scripture. For if this authority is regarded as a debatable point, one can still speak of the tradition of the Lord's Supper, but it will be difficult to continue ascribing to the Supper that significance by which it gives us assurance of faith.[43]

Berkouwer refers to the words of the institution in Matthew, Mark, Luke, and Paul. However, he does not speak of the differing versions, the additions and subtractions which have accumulated in the various texts. He merely states: "All these passages have decisively determined the practice and confession of the church regarding the Lord's Supper." At no time does he attempt to resolve the conflict between the Synoptics, in which Jesus eats the Passover, and John's account, in which the meal is eaten before the Passover. This radical difference is completely ignored.

What All of This Means to a Believer in the Book of Mormon

The purpose of this whole review of the metamorphosis in theological attitudes toward the Lord's Supper is to enable us to draw a meaningful and definite conclusion about this important sacrament. Certainly, if we were to depend only on the New Testament record in trying to find meaning for this observance, we would not be any wiser than those who have wrestled with the problem for over a hundred years.

The whole issue hinges on what Christ did and said at the last meal he ate with his disciples (assuming that he actually ate one). There is no consensus thus far on the part of scholars. As Latter Day Saints and believers in the Book of Mormon, however, we have some additional information which may be relevant. We believe that as well as visiting the known world of his time, Christ made a visit to this hemisphere. His actions and teachings on this land are recorded, just as his actions and teachings were recorded when he visited Palestine. Do they shed light on the subject? It is this that we will investigate in the next chapter.

---

1. Matthew 26:17-18.
2. Mark 14:12.
3. Mark 14:16.
4. Luke 22:15.
5. Exodus 12:1-28.
6. Deuteronomy 16:6.

7. Exodus 6:6-8.
8. See also William Barclay, *The Lord's Supper*, *op. cit.*, pp. 20-24.
9. Matthew 26:47.
10. Luke 22:66 f.
11. William Barclay, *The Lord's Supper*, *op. cit.*, pp. 28, 29.
12. John 13:1-3.
13. John 19:14.
14. John 18:28.
15. Luke 22:66.
16. *The Dead Sea Scrolls and Primitive Christianity*, a Mentor Omega Book, p. 27.
17. William Barclay, *The Lord's Supper*, *op. cit.*, p. 28.
18. I Corinthians 11:24.
19. Luke 22:19.
20. I Corinthians 11:25.
21. Luke 22:20.
22. I Corinthians 11:23.
23. *Justin Martyr's First Apology*, Antenicene Christian Library, Edinburgh.
24. *Justin Martyr's First Apology*, *op. cit.*
25. *Justin Martyr*, by Basil Gildersleeve, Harper Brothers, 1877, p. 198.
26. *The Body of Christ*, John Murray, London, 1909, pp. 6-7.
27. *The Rise of Christianity*, Longman's, London, 1948.
28. Gore, *The Body of Christ*, *op. cit.*, p. 289.
29. Barnes, *The Rise of Christianity*, *op. cit.*, p. 326.
30. *Ibid.*, p. 327.
31. *Ibid.*, p. 251.
32. *Ibid.*, p. 281.
33. *Ibid.*, p. 289.
34. *Eusebius Ecclesiastical History*, Chapter XXII, Book IV; Chapters VIII and XXVIII, Box V. (Also read item D, Marcion's Gospel, *Interpreter's Bible*, Vol. 8, p. 22.)
35. Text and Ancient Versions of the New Testament, *Interpreter's Bible*, Vol. 1, pp. 72-83.
36. *Interpreter's Bible*, Vol. 7, Section X, p. 244.
37. William Barclay, *The Lord's Supper*, *op. cit.*, p. 35.
38. Timothy 3:16; II Peter 1:20,21.
39. William Barclay, *The Lord's Supper*, "The Meaning of Today," Chapter 6.
40. *The Sacrament: An Experiment in Ecumenical Honesty*, Abingdon Press, 1969.
41. *Ibid.*, pp. 77-78.
42. *Ibid.*, p. 79.
43. *The Sacraments*, William B. Erdman Publishing Co., Grand Rapids, Mich., 1969, pp. 189-190.

CHAPTER THREE

IN SEARCH OF AUTHORITY

A first glance at the Book of Mormon account of the Lord's Supper appears to be unimpressive. This is so because many of the popular statements connected with this sacrament as found in the Synoptic accounts are not found in the Book of Mormon. Tradition and long usage of the New Testament cause a distrust of that which is different from that to which we are accustomed. An in-depth study, however, reveals another story. Many of the words that have been hallowed by constant usage, such as "Passover" and "covenant," are not found in the Book of Mormon. (It is interesting to note that these words are now being contested by the critics.) Its language appears to be akin to the Lord's Supper discourse recorded by John. This similarity with the fourth gospel does not assist in removing the distrust, particularly since the Gospel of John is not held with deep esteem by some Bible critics. But the differences and similarities appear to be productive when a detailed study is made.

The one cardinal point which should be kept in mind as comparisons are begun is the date of biblical criticisms. Its modern origin dates from the middle of the third decade of the nineteenth century when David Fredrich Strauss published his *Life of Jesus*. By that time the account of the Lord's Supper in the Book of Mormon was already in print; thus it came ahead of this criticism and was not influenced by it.

Likewise the corruption in the gospel text which was discovered in the previous chapter was anticipated in the Book of Mormon and preceded Form Criticism by about twenty years.[1] This is amazing since the untarnished authority of the New Testament was beyond question at the time. This precedence is indeed prophetic.

Book of Mormon Account

On the first day of the Lord's visit to this hemisphere, ten important things occurred, and among them was the serving of the Lord's Supper. All of these are recorded in three chapters of III Nephi:

1. Jesus introduced himself.[2]
2. He called and instructed the twelve disciples.[3]
3. He addressed the multitude regarding his mission and repeated the sermon on the mount.[4]
4. He gave additional instructions to the twelve disciples.[5]
5. He continued to instruct the multitude.[6]
6. He gave a discourse on the Law of Moses.[7]
7. He provided more elucidation to the twelve disciples, this time on "the other sheep."[8]
8. After giving additional instruction to the multitude, he healed the sick and blessed the children.[9]
9. He directed the serving of the Lord's Supper.[10]
10. He ordained the twelve disciples, then departed for the day.[11]

Particular attention is given to these events because they seem to sum up his purpose and mission. The disputations which took place between him and the Jews in Palestine do not appear here; neither do the parables that he gave when he was in Palestine. His miraculous descent, coupled with prophecies given by the Nephite prophets of his visit to the Americas, was enough to give his presence the authority it needed. Because of this ready acceptance, he immediately entered into the discussion and enactment of the very essence of his mission. Fundamental among these teachings was the serving of and instructions regarding the Communion. Had this been of little or no value, he would not have mentioned it. Because of its vital significance to his total objective, however, it was included in the activities of that first day.

To further emphasize the supreme value and function of this sacrament in the life of his disciples as it relates to the performance of their church duties, it was served again on the following day.[12] This time the bread and wine appeared miraculously.

The Actual Serving

Details of the enactment of the Supper are recorded in the eighth chapter of III Nephi. Following instructions to the twelve disciples and to the multitude, the bread is served:[13]

And it came to pass that Jesus commanded his disciples that they should bring forth some bread and wine unto him. And while they were gone for bread and wine, he commanded the multitude that they should sit themselves down upon the earth. And when the disciples had come with bread and wine, he took of the bread, and break and blessed it; and he gave unto the disciples, and commanded that they should eat. And when they had eat [sic], and were filled, he

71

commanded that they should give unto the multitude.[14]

And when the multitude had eaten and were filled, he said unto the disciples, Behold, there shall one be ordained among you, and to him will I give power that he shall break bread, and bless it, and give unto the people of my church, unto all those who shall believe and be baptized in my name. And this shall ye always observe to do, even as I have done, even as I have broken bread, and blessed it, and gave it unto you. And this shall ye do in remembrance of my body, which I have shewn unto you. And it shall be a testimony unto the Father, that ye do always remember me. And if ye do always remember me, ye shall have my Spirit to be with you.

Of the wine, it is written:

And it came to pass that when he had said these words, he commanded his disciples that they should take of the wine of the cup, and drink of it, and that they should also give unto the multitude, that they might drink of it. And it came to pass that they did so, and did drink of it, and were filled; and they gave unto the multitude, and they did drink, and they were filled. And when the disciples had done this, Jesus said unto them, Blessed are ye for this thing which ye have done, for this is fulfilling my commandments, and this doth witness unto the Father that ye are willing to do that which I have commanded you. And this shall ye always do unto those who repent and are baptized in my name; and ye shall do it in remembrance of my blood, which I have shed for you, that ye may witness unto the Father that ye do always remember me. And if ye do always remember me, ye shall have my Spirit to be with you.

The same chapter contains this admonition and advice:

Behold, verily, verily I say unto you, I give unto you another commandment, and then I must go unto my Father, that I may fulfill other commandments which he hath given me. And now behold, this is the commandment which I give unto you, that ye shall not suffer any one knowingly, to partake of my flesh and blood unworthily, when ye shall minister it, for whoso eateth and drinketh my flesh and blood unworthily, eateth and drinketh damnation to his soul; therefore if ye know that a man is unworthy to eat and drink of my flesh and blood, ye shall forbid him; nevertheless ye shall not cast him out from among you, but ye shall minister unto him, and shall pray for him unto the Father, in my name. And if it so be that he repenteth, and is baptized in my name, then shall ye receive him, and shall minister unto him of my flesh and blood.

The Passover Issue

The overriding question is the Passover issue. Connecting the Lord's Supper with the Jewish Passover, such as the Synoptics do, has raised insolvable problems. These are multiplied, however, if we are to accept the authority of John. The outcome of this confusion is a theological hesitancy among scholars which raises suspicions, thus alienating the ordinary Christian and destroying the meaning and efficacy of this sacrament. Placed in such an authoritative vacuum, we have no choice but to look "to the author and finisher of our faith." If Jesus is the one who authored this sacrament, he should be able to remove the uncertainty and turn it to an immutable belief. And he has. The word "Passover" does not appear in his teaching on the Americas. Its absence from the institution on this hemisphere gives authority to the accuracy of John's account concerning the Lord's Supper. This in turn supports the divine claim behind the Book of Mormon.

The omission, both in John and III Nephi, of the word "Passover" may be difficult to accept by those who base their belief on the long heritage of the wording in the King James version. This is understandable, and one may wonder as to how this word entered into the Synoptic text. There is the strong possibility that its inclusion came as a backlash against the teachings of the Marcionites who attempted to divorce Christianity from any connection with Judaism and the Old Testament.[15] This struggle was forgotten by theologians but surfaced again in the second quarter of the nineteenth century. The man responsible for this was Ferdinand Christian Baur, a theological professor at the

University of Tubingen in Germany. His discovery of Marcion's writings brought him to the conclusion that there were two parties in the apostolic and post-apostolic church—the Jewish Christian and the Gentile Christian. Paul championed the Gentile Christian foundation. Baur rejected Paul's authorship of the pastoral epistles, and attributed them to other second century Christian writers who attempted to smooth the conflict between the two. He even rejected the present authorship of the fourth gospel. Williston Walker refers to Marcion as the "first church reformer."[16] The Synoptics, though written before the destruction of the second temple, were still transmitted by traditions in the second century in widely separated Christian localities. As the traditions were put into writing, those believing in the Jewish Christian foundation may have inserted the term "Passover" in good faith believing that Christ had uttered the word. Christ, however, did not refer to the last meal with the twelve as the Passover. For this we have the combined authority of John and the Book of Mormon.

The New Covenant

The question of the covenant is more complicated than the Passover problem. The word "covenant" is omitted from the short manuscript of Luke, but appears in Matthew, Mark, long Luke, and Paul. The omission of the word from the shorter Luke and its appearance in the longer text arouses the suspicion with students that the word is of a later addition when the idea of the covenant was gaining hold on tradition. Is the same true of Matthew, Mark, and Paul's accounts? No one can hazard a guess. This leaves the Christian world in a

74

quandary, depending on whimsical notions.

The discovery that the word "new" was a later addition to the original of Matthew and Mark adds to the suspicion. Furthermore, as was pointed out in the previous chapter, the Revised Standard Version of the Bible popularizes the confusion by placing the unresolved question in the hands of anyone who desires to read. In it the word "covenant" is omitted from Luke's account,[17] and "new" from Matthew and Mark's accounts.[18] In the New English Bible, translated nine years later, the same thing was done. Where is the layman or the theologian who can make a meaningful and worshipful practice of a sacrament when over its wording hangs the element of doubt?

Of deeper interest now is, what does the fourth gospel say on this issue? The son of Zebedee is the only one of the four evangelists who gives a lengthy account of what the Lord said after eating the sacred meal with the twelve disciples (here called the Lord's Supper discourse). It covers the thirteenth through the seventeenth chapters of his gospel. The word "covenant" as such does not appear in these pages. The idea of a covenant, however, is shot through and through its message. One of the essential features of this discourse is the promise of the Lord's presence in those who ate the meal with him. Yet there is a paradox in this declaration when one considers that not long before Christ made this statement he had announced his death.[19] "Yet a little while," he said, "and the world seeth me no more; but ye see me: because I live, ye shall live also. At that day ye shall know that I am in my Father, and ye in me, and I in you."[20] How will he be in them? The answer he gives is this: "He that hath my commandments, and keepeth them, he it is that loveth me; and he that loveth me shall be loved of my Father, and I will love him, and will manifest myself to him."[21] The manifestation spoken of here is his spiritual presence with them. What is worthy of note is that this presence is conditional. You keep my commandment, words, and sayings, which are truths, and you will be rewarded with my spiritual presence. Ignore them and the promise becomes null and void. This is the essence of the covenant.

The language of this discourse may still be difficult to understand. On two separate occasions the twelve sought for clarification.[22] The Lord answered every question, and the answer which covers all is the one given to Peter in the previous chapter: "What I do thou knowest not now; but thou shalt know hereafter."[23] After his physical resurrection and Pentecost, the puzzle was cleared, and they knew what he meant. Though he was invisible to the eyes of men, he was made visible to their eyes and souls. Immediately after these two separate experiences, the words, commandments, and sayings of the Lord became living flesh. Without the atonement, resurrection, and the Holy Spirit, there would have been no covenant, and the words, sayings, and commandments of the Lord would have been forgotten.

Let us see now if the Book of Mormon confirms what John wrote. As we study the observance of this meal on this hemisphere, we discover that, as in the Gospel of John, the word "covenant" is not mentioned in the Book of Mormon. But the similarity does not end here. As John's account insists on the commandments, so does the Book of Mormon account. Jesus said, "Blessed are ye for this thing which ye have done, for this is fulfilling my commandments, and this doth witness unto the Father that ye are willing to do that which I have commanded you."[24] This may be interpreted to mean obedience to the commandment of serving the emblems. But obedience in this one particular case is an evidence of obedience to other commandments previously given.

Likewise, the consecration prayer he taught them to be said over the bread petitions that they "always remember him, and keep his commandments which he hath given them."[25] The memory of the Lord is here linked to the keeping of his commandments. Had we not the knowledge that the Book of Mormon was first published in 1829, it would be easy for us to surmise that both accounts were written by one individual.

"And Were Filled"

If the observance of the Lord's Supper in the Book of Mormon had been suggested by the action and current beliefs of the community where Joseph Smith lived, the words "and were filled" would not have appeared. No one in the early 1800s or since—looked at the Lord's Supper as a full-course meal. Such a meal was mentioned only in the second chapter of Acts and the eleventh chapter of I Corinthians. Another place where a full meal is observed as the Lord's Supper is mentioned in the *Didache*. In the opening words of chapter ten of this manual are these words: "And after you are satisfied with food, thus give thanks." This booklet was still lost when the Book of Mormon was written. The debate continues as to the nature of this meal mentioned in the *Didache*. Was it the full meal of Jewish Shaburah or the Kiddush? There is no need for debate about the meal in the Book of Mormon, however. It was the meal of the Lord—"his flesh and blood"—and he ate it with 2,500 guests present. He did not identify it with either one of the Jewish meals, including the Passover. It was *his* meal, the Lord's Supper. This was observed first as a full-course meal in Jerusalem, Corinth, and Antioch, where the *Didache* is supposed to have been written, and in the Western Hemisphere as recorded in the Book of Mormon.

"Believe and Be Baptized"

Baptism and the Lord's Supper are not connected with each other in the New Testament. Depending on this account only we cannot say that the twelve apostles with whom the Lord observed this meal were baptized. Those who partook of it, mentioned in the second chapter of Acts, were baptized.[26] But this could have been an incident and no more. Only in the Book of Mormon and in *Justin Martyr's First Apology* was baptism made a prerequisite to the Lord's Supper. Justin wrote:

> And this food is called among us the Eucharist, of which no one is allowed to partake but the man who believes that the things which we teach are true, and who has been washed with the washing that is for the remission of sins.

It is remarkable how the statement connecting baptism with the Lord's Supper in the Book of Mormon agrees precisely with that of Justin. Joseph Smith, at his age and educational attainment, could not have been acquainted with *Justin Martyr's Apology*. This fact alone supports the divine origin of the sacrament. Here for the first time we discover close Communion.

What Did Jesus Teach?

According to tradition in the early church, Jesus taught and practiced close Communion. Those who ate the meal in II Acts were baptized Jews. This practice persisted even among the reformers. Lately, however, under the uncertainty produced by the critical investigation of the Lord's Supper, many who held to close Communion are now advocating the opposite. This trend has already caught up with some in our church, and their advocacy of open Communion has become common knowledge. Those favoring it are few, but they are knowledgeable of the rationale on which modern Christian theologians base their conclusions.

The Book of Mormon account is specific:

> ...And this shall ye always do unto those who repent and are baptized in my name; and ye shall do it in remembrance of my blood.[27] ...And now behold, this is the commandment which I give unto you, that ye shall not suffer anyone knowingly, to partake of my flesh and blood unworthily. ... Therefore if ye know that a man is unworthy to eat and drink of my flesh and blood, ye shall forbid him. ...And if it so be that he repenteth, and is baptized in my name, then shall ye receive him, and shall minister unto him of my flesh and blood.[28]

The responsibility of rejection rests with the officiating minister. The unbaptized has no choice.

This statement, however, clear as it is, does not remove all objections, and some continue to argue the point that Christ served the Lord's Supper to those who were not baptized. This is true in only one sense. The 2,500 participating in that meal were not baptized. Furthermore, baptism did not enter into the picture until after the twelve disciples were ordained.[29] Later they were baptized.[30] Here again we notice another reversal of the ordinary sequence of events—ordination before baptism.

79

This action on the part of our Lord cannot be taken by the serious-minded as a criterion for either open Communion or ordination before baptism. Procedures followed when Christ was personally present do not contravene a command to be observed during his bodily absence. We have a good example of this in the question which was put to him by the disciples of John concerning fasting. Apparently his own disciples did not fast, but the Pharisees and John's disciples did. The answer he gave them is revealing: "Can the children of the bridechamber mourn, as long as the bridegroom is with them? But the days will come when the bridegroom shall be taken from them, and then shall they fast."[31]

If we are to apply the argument of the open Communion advocates to the answer given the disciples of John, then we will conclude by saying that Christ did not believe in fasting—a preposterous idea.

It is interesting to follow the exegesis made on the foregoing text by Sherman E. Johnson in the *Interpreter's Bible:*

Jesus. . . reminds his hearers that no one fasts as long as a marriage feast is going on; at such a time the guests were dispensed from certain religious duties, and even rabbis were expected to forsake the study of the law. But this is not all. Jewish teaching often described "the days of the Messiah" with the figure of a wedding feast; and Jesus and his disciples in their life together already enjoy a foretaste. . . in Jesus' mighty deeds.

Likewise, there was no need for baptism before partaking of the Lord's Supper for those who witnessed his majestic descent on this hemisphere.

Those who object to close Communion should first know the meaning of the bread and wine in this sacrament. "My flesh and blood" are used as symbols of the body of Christ. They are not the very substance of the flesh and blood of the Lord. A symbol is a visible sign of something invisible. From the days of St. Augustine to the days of Zwingli and Calvin and even down to the present, the bread and wine have been used by Protestants as symbols of the body of Christ. St. Augustine said: "In them [the bread and wine] one thing is seen and another thing is understood." What we see with our eyes is bread and wine, but what we understand spiritually is that we are in the presence of the invisible Lord.

The same is true of baptism, the symbol of burial and resurrection into a new life with Christ.[32] The symbol, however, loses its meaning before the One who was slain, buried, arose from the grave, ascended into heaven, then descended to stand before the eyes of 2,500 people. This action on the part of the Lord, however, does not contravene his command that one needs to be baptized before partaking of the bread and wine when the Lord is absent in the body.

Theological support for what already has been stated is given by a noted Roman Catholic theologian, Edward Schillebeeckx.

... by his ascension the "primordial sacrament" leaves the world, the economy of the "separated sacraments" becomes operative in consequence of the incarnation and as its prolongation. From Scripture we learn that while none of the twelve Apostles who enjoyed immediate contact with the "primordial sacrament" himself was baptized, St. Paul, the "thirteenth Apostle," who had not encountered the earthly Christ in faith, was in fact baptized. Sacramentality thus bridges the gap and solves the disproportion between the Christ of heaven and unglorified humanity, and makes possible a reciprocal human encounter of Christ and men even after the ascension. ...[33]

If we accept the reasoning of Schillebeeckx as being

sound, those who witnessed the descent of the physical Christ on this hemisphere encountered the primordial sacrament, and like the original twelve at Jerusalem had no need of further sacramentality through baptism. But like Paul who had not encountered the earthly Christ in the flesh and thus had need of the sacrament of baptism, those who did not witness his descent on this hemisphere need the sacrament of baptism before partaking of the Lord's Supper.

There is another misunderstood point on which the advocates of open Communion base their conclusion or judgment; one individual has no right to judge another.[34] The Corinthians to whom Paul was writing were the church in Corinth—people who were already baptized. The judgment he speaks of was not over whether they were or were not baptized. It was a judgment over conduct at the Lord's table, and included with it judgment over secret motives and sinful acts which resulted in contention, divisions, and heresies.[35]

The Book of Mormon account is completely different. The Lord limited judgment to baptism only. The church has the right to judge whether the desiring participant is baptized or not. We, however, have no right to judge his or her secret attitude or sinful behavior after baptism. God is the only judge. In extreme cases of flagrant disregard to the teaching of the Lord the church is given the right to judge.[36]

Those desiring to see the Lord's Supper administered to good people who are not members of the church are not fully acquainted with the purpose of baptism as taught in the Book of Mormon. Baptism, briefly stated, is a covenant.[37] The Lord's Supper, accepted by one who has not covenanted with Christ to keep his

82

commandments, is a meaningless ceremony devoid of any sacramental significance.

The Missing Prayer Is Found

Reference has already been made in the previous chapter to Justin Martyr's "Prayer of His Word," and to the elation it engendered in the hearts of theologians when the *Didache* was discovered. But disappointment also ensued when the prayer proved not to be the prayer the Lord pronounced on the emblems. Since the search has been futile, modern students make no mention of it. When reference is now made to prayers on the elements it is usually to the "First Eucharistic prayers"—then a qualifying statement "in the *Didache*."[38] The qualification is purposely and honestly made so as not to mislead the reader in assuming that the prayer in the *Didache* is the prayer the Lord uttered as he consecrated the emblems in the upper room.

Those who study the enactment of the Lord's Supper on this continent discover a prayer of blessing spoken by the Lord on the emblems with instruction to repeat.[39]

Of special interest to us is the independent origin of the Book of Mormon account from both Justin Martyr's work and that of the *Didache*. It would be the height of credulity to assume that the writer of the Book of Mormon was acquainted with Justin Martyr's "Prayer of His Word" and penned this prayer to aid or confound the critic even before biblical criticism became widespread. Also, the *Didache* was not discovered until years after the Book of Mormon was printed. So, in the absence of the slightest hint of human craftiness and scheming, we have to contend with the fact that the prayer in the Book of Mormon is of divine origin. Also it is difficult to escape from the conclusion which follows—namely, that Christ visited the new world after his resurrection from the grave in the old.

One still has to deal with such extremely radical views as those held by Barnes. Justin wrote, "There appears to have been no set form of consecration prayers."[40] His argument here, of course, is with the proponents of transubstantiation who felt the change in the substance of the bread and wine could have been tied to the prayer the Lord taught the twelve to pray on the elements. In support of his extreme views, Barnes in his translation of Justin Martyr's First Apology differs materially from other translations. For the "Prayer of His Word" he substitutes the "prayer of the Logos" thus removing the pronoun "his." This is the stand on which he bases his rejection of any set form of consecration prayer made by the Lord (reference pp. 29-31).

In all fairness to Barnes, there are those who feel that Justin's statement is capable of being translated either way.[41] In this case there is a deadlock between the disputants. Modern students ignore the statement. Its influence as an exhibit supporting the institution has been compromised—but not so in this study. There is a consecration prayer taught by Christ to his disciples in the Americas to be used over the elements. Its presence preceded biblical criticisms which brought Justin's statement to light in support of the Eucharist and could not have been influenced by the critics' debate. Its independent nature supports the soundness of the earlier translation made of Justin's Greek original, namely, "by the prayer of his word"—the prayer Christ taught.

The Prayer Testifies of Its Source

The prayer is *not* lost. Its divine credentials are woven

into the fabric of its simple and brief language, but in order for us to arrive at this conclusion we must first study the prayer. Second, since the prayer is claimed to be of divine origin, we should compare it with other prayers attributed to the Lord. And, third, we should make the same comparison with some of the oldest consecration prayers available. Only by taking this lengthy approach can we arrive at a reasoned judgment. Here is the prayer on the bread:

O God, the eternal Father, we ask thee in the name of thy Son Jesus Christ, to bless and sanctify this bread to the souls of all those who partake of it, that they may eat in remembrance of the body of thy Son, and witness unto thee, O God the eternal Father, that they are willing to take upon them the name of thy Son, and always remember him, and keep his commandments which he hath given them, that they may always have his Spirit to be with them. Amen.[42]

The prayer on the wine is similar:

O God, the eternal Father, we ask thee in the name of thy Son Jesus Christ, to bless and sanctify this wine to the souls of all those who drink of it, that they may do it in remembrance of the blood of thy Son which was shed for them, that they may witness unto thee, O God, the eternal Father, that they do always remember him, that they may have his Spirit to be with them. Amen.[43]

Moroni wanted us to know that his people "administered it according to the commandments of Christ," and they did it kneeling.[44] He does not say that the words are the words of Christ, but the term "commandments" carries with it not only the act of kneeling but also the wording. This view is strengthened by the ordination prayer of the twelve disciples. Before recording the prayer Moroni wrote that these were "the words of Christ, which he spake unto his disciples, the twelve whom he had chosen."[45] If the wording of the ordination came from Christ, the wording of the consecration prayer on the emblems must have come

85

from him also. So the prayer is the prayer which Justin Martyr tells us is the "Prayer of His Word."

We are fortunate indeed in having two prayers uttered by Christ while he was in Judea; the Lord's prayer[46] and the consecration prayer of the Twelve.[47] If the missing but now-found prayer used on the elements in the Book of Mormon is from him, it should compare favorably with the other two spoken in Judea.

The Lord's prayers quoted in Matthew and Luke differ in composition but retain the same substance. Matthew's prayer has seven petitions, while that recorded by Luke has only three.[48] Some think that editorial insertions may have entered into the text of the one by Matthew; even so, the prayer is noted for its simplicity, scope of coverage, and economy in wording. The same thing can be rightly said of the consecration prayer in the Book of Mormon. Instead of seven, it has only four petitions:

1. It asks the heavenly Father to "bless and sanctify" the bread and wine.
2. The bread and wine are to be taken in remembrance of the "body of thy Son," and of his blood "which was shed for them."
3. In the case of the bread, "remembrance" is of the Son and of his commandments.
4. The whole purpose is that the participants may have "his Spirit to be with them."

It contains the same simplicity, economy of words, and scope of coverage as the biblical Lord's prayer.

The comparison is much more favorable when we take into consideration the consecration prayer uttered by the Lord on the Twelve while in the upper room in Jerusalem. The prayer reads:

I have given them thy word; and the world hath hated them, because they are not of the world, even as I am not of the world. I pray not that thou shouldest take them out of the world, but that thou shouldest keep them from the evil. They are not of the world, even as I am not of the world. Sanctify them through thy truth; thy word is truth. As thou hast sent me into the world, even so have I also sent them into the world. And for their sakes I sanctify myself, that they also may be sanctified through the truth.

Note should be made of the substantive issues: "sanctification" and the "word." It is marvelous how identical these words are with the words of the first and third petition of the prayer of the blessing on the emblems. The first petition asks for sanctification, and the third one pleads for the continued memory of Christ and his commandments. Again, a rich connection exists between the Book of Mormon account of the Supper and the Johannine happenings in the upper room at Jerusalem.

Consecration Prayer Compared with the *Didache*

The beauty and divinity of this prayer are more apparent when compared with other prayers on the subject. First we shall consider the two prayers which fired the imagination of students nearly a century ago, only to cause disappointment when examined more carefully—the prayers in the *Didache* (translation by Krisopp Lake).

Chapter 9:
 1. And concerning the Eucharist, hold the Eucharist thus:
 2. First concerning the cup, We give thanks to thee, Our Father, for the Holy Vine of David, thy child, which, thou didst make known to us through Jesus thy Child; to thee be glory for ever.
 3. And concerning the broken bread; We give thee thanks, Our Father, for the life and knowledge which thou didst make known to us through Jesus thy Child. To thee be glory for ever.
 4. As this broken bread was scattered upon the mountains, but was brought together and became one, so let thy Church be

gathered together from the ends of the earth into thy kingdom, for thine is the glory and the power through Jesus Christ for ever.

5. But let none eat or drink of your Eucharist except those who have been baptized in the Lord's name. For concerning this also did the Lord say, "Give not that which is holy to the dogs."

Chapter 10:
1. But after you are satisfied with food, thus give thanks:
2. We give thanks to thee, O Holy Father, for thy Holy Name which thou didst make to tabernacle in our hearts, and for the knowledge and faith and immortality which thou didst make known to us through Jesus thy Holy Child. To thee be glory for ever.
3. Thou, Lord Almighty, didst create all things for thy name's sake, and didst give food and drink to men for their enjoyment, that they might give thanks to thee, but us hast thou blessed with spiritual food and drink and eternal light through thy Child.
4. Above all we give thanks to thee for that thou art Almighty. To thee be glory for ever.
5. Remember, Lord, thy Church, to deliver it from all evil and to make it Perfect in thy love, and gather it together in its holiness from the four winds to thy kingdom which thou has prepared for it. For thine is the power and the glory for ever.
6. Let grace come and let this world pass away. Hosannah to the God of David. If any man be holy let him come! If any man be not, let him repent: Maran Atha! Amen. [The words "Maran Atha are Aramaic, meaning, "Our Lord, Come."]

It is easily seen that the prayer of chapter 9 is a prayer of thanksgiving and not a prayer of blessing. The second prayer is clearly a benedictory prayer. There is also in it the expression of thanksgiving as well. It is far removed from a prayer of blessing.

The Prayer Compared with Ancient Liturgy

The word "liturgy" is not in common use in our church, but the prayer of the Lord which we pray on the emblems is liturgical and the first of its kind. The word "liturgy" means corporate worship, and in the early period of its usage it was always connected with the Lord's Supper. There is a wider meaning given to it now which covers almost all acts of corporate Christian worship. Here we use it in the strict original sense and not in the modern one. According to the Book of Mormon account of the Lord's Supper, Christ introduced the first liturgical service when he gave the prayer under discussion and ordered the participants to kneel as it was read. Somehow this prayer was lost, and in its absence other liturgical forms came into being. It is time now to compare this divinely given liturgy with man-made liturgies. This is not to show the inferiority of other liturgies but to reveal the original source of liturgy. The primary concern is Christ and this sacrament.

Ancient liturgies appeared in different localities, and some were considered of apostolic source. Now we know differently.

The three liturgies we shall consider here belong to the Egyptian Rite, or the liturgies of St. Mark. They are taken from the excellent book, *The Mystery of Sacrifice*, by Evelyn Underhill.[49]

O Lord our God, we have set before thy sight thine own of thine own gifts; and we pray and beseech thee, O good Lord and Lover of men, send forth from thy holy height, from thine appointed dwelling place, from thy bosom that embraces all, the very Paraclete, the Spirit of Truth, the Holy One, the Lord and Lifegiver; who spake by the law and by the prophets and apostles, who is everywhere present and filleth all things; working at his own and not another's bidding, in those whom he willeth the Hallowing which is pleasing in thy sight. One in nature, manifold in working, fountain of heavenly grace, of one substance with thee, who proceedeth from thee.... Look upon us and send thine Holy Spirit upon this bread and upon this cup, that he may sanctify and perfect them, as being God all-powerful, and make this bread the Body and this cup the

Blood of the new covenant of our Lord Jesus Christ.—Liturgy of St. Mark.

We pray and beseech thee, O Holy of Holies, in the good pleasure of thy bounty, that thy Holy Spirit may come down upon us and upon these gifts set forth before thee, and bless them and hallow them and make this bread to be indeed the previous Body of our Lord and God and Saviour Jesus Christ. And this cup to be indeed the Previous Blood of our Lord and God and Saviour Jesus Christ, which was poured out for the life and salvation of the world. And do thou unite us, who are partakers of the one Bread and one Cup, one with another in the fellowship of One Holy Spirit, and cause none of us to partake of the Holy Body and Blood of thy Christ unto judgment or condemnation, but that we may find mercy and grace with all thy Saints, who from old have been well-pleasing unto thee.—Liturgy of St. Basil

In the same night in which thou didst deliver thyself up of thine own power, taking bread in thy holy pure and spotless hands, thou didst look up to thine own Father, our God and the God of all. Thou didst give thanks, bless, sanctify and break, and gavest to thy holy disciples and apostles, saying: Take, eat: this is my Body which is broken for you and for many, and is given for the remission of sins: Do this for my memorial. Likewise, after supper, thou didst take the cup and didst mix it with the fruit of the vine and water; thou didst give thanks, bless, sanctify, and gavest to thy holy disciples and apostles, saying: Drink ye all of it: this is my Blood of the new covenant, which is shed for you and for many for the remission of sins. Do this for my memorial. For as often as ye eat this bread and drink this cup ye proclaim my death and confess my resurrection until I come.

Therefore, O Lord, mindful of thy descent upon earth, and thy lifegiving death, thy three-days burial and thy resurrection from the dead, thy ascension into heaven, and sitting down on the right hand of the Father, and thy coming from the heavens, thy terrible and glorious second coming, we offer to thee thine own of thine own gifts, for all, through all, and in all.—Coptic Liturgy

In general these prayers are lengthy and full of laudatory adjectives, but omit commitments to the words, sayings, and commandments of Christ. The prayers differ in substance from the prayer of blessing the Lord pronounced while in America. There is a remote similarity between these prayers and the ones

90

Christ uttered; however, there is considerable similarity between his prayer of blessing on the emblems and the consecration prayer pronounced on the Twelve in Judea.

One Ordained

The Synoptics make no mention of the requirement for a specially ordained individual to administer this sacrament, though Luke calls for its repetition. As Christ administered it to the Nephites on this hemisphere, he said: "There shall one be ordained among you, and to him will I give power that he shall break bread, and bless it."[50] John's account on the other hand, is different. It appears that ordination was required, not only to administer the sacrament but in speaking for Christ. "I have chosen you," he writes, "and ordained you, that ye should go and bring forth fruit, and that your fruit should remain."[51] The only difference is that ordination had already taken place in Judea but was not yet consummated here. John's statement was made in the middle of the Lord's Supper discourse, and the statement in III Nephi was made while Christ inaugurated the Supper on this hemisphere.

"Remember Him and Keep His Commandments"

The idea of "do this in remembrance of me" comes from Luke and the writings of Paul. These words dominate the thinking and influence the worship of all Christians who revere this sacrament. The fact of remembrance appears in the Book of Mormon as well. It is mentioned twice in the prayer of blessing on the bread, but with a slight and very important addition:

"Always remember him, and keep his commandments which he hath given them."

Depending on Luke's and Paul's accounts only, Christian worship tends to lean toward the adoration of Christ as it did during the dark ages. This is not to be critical of adoration in worship. Adoration is necessary for true worship as we link the message of Christ with the memory of his person. Christianity was robbed of its dynamics when it laid the emphasis on the Redeemer and ignored the redeeming message. As the Lord inaugurated the Lord's Supper in the Americas, he added to his personal remembrance the remembrance of his "commandments" which cover the religious, moral, and social duties of man.

The Johannine discourse of the Lord's Supper does not ignore the commandments. The word "remembrance" is not used in this account. The allegory of the vine, the vine dresser, and the branches, however,[52] suggests a cohesion that is stronger than remembrance. Such language as: "if ye abide in me, and my words abide in you" and "If ye keep my commandments, ye shall abide in my love, even as I have kept my Father's commandments, and abide in his love,"[53] is precious and needs to be emphasized today wherever the Lord's Supper is served. This is one of the contributions of the Book of Mormon to modern Christianity.

Presence of the Spirit

Participation in the Lord's Supper implies a personal commitment. Part of this commitment is implicit at this juncture of the study, but the other part is quite explicit—the dedication to the memory of the Lord and the observance of his commandments. Keeping these

92

words and making them flesh is not a simple task. Of the early disciples it demanded terrible sacrifice which at times ended in martyrdom. A task involving such hardships is not easily borne without the presence of the Spirit. Hence the consecration prayer over the elements concludes with: "that they may have his Spirit to be with them. Amen." As we commit ourselves to the keeping of the commandments we do so with the assurance that the Spirit which sustained him in the hour of his greatest difficulty will also sustain us.

The Synoptics contain no such promise of assistance in the wording of the Lord's Supper. Only John, in his Lord's Supper discourse, makes such a promise: "I will pray the Father, and he shall give you the Conforter, that he may abide with you for ever."[54] This promise is conditional, depending on the keeping of the "commandments," "words," and "sayings" of Christ.[55] This is in keeping with the Israelitish covenant.[56] The promise is not limited to the words of the fourteenth chapter but appears throughout this discourse. Anyone keeping the covenant needs the assistance of his spirit.

Again, a perfect harmony exists between the Book of Mormon account of the Lord's Supper and John's account of the same meal.

A Puzzling Discovery

As we try to sum up the teaching of the Book of Mormon on the Lord's Supper we come face-to-face with a significant discovery—the harmony between it and the Johannine writing. This similarity cannot be called incidental. On the questionable issues thus far covered there are six agreements:

1. The critics reject the Synoptic claim to a Passover

meal and agree with John.

The Book of Mormon account does not mention a Passover, and again is in concurrence with John's account.

2. Some critics doubt the Synoptic assertion that the meal is a covenant. John infers such a covenant. The Book of Mormon account does not mention it either but infers it quite strongly.

3. Neither John nor the Synoptics mention a prayer uttered by the Lord on the emblems. This prayer is first mentioned by Justin Martyr. The Book of Mormon has such a prayer, and its repetition is commanded by the Lord. The prayer, furthermore, compares favorably with the consecration prayer uttered by Christ on the Twelve and recorded only by John.

4. The Book of Mormon is very specific concerning who is authorized to administer this sacrament—"one ordained." The Synoptics do not mention ordination in this connection. John, in the Lord's Supper discourse, mentions the fact that Christ "chose and ordained" men for priestly service.

5. The Book of Mormon adds keeping the "commandments" to the memory of Christ. Luke and Paul are united on the "remembrance" of Jesus but ignore the remembrance of the "commandments." John infers the memory of Christ but insists on keeping the commandments and, on this feature, agrees with the Book of Mormon.

6. Both the Johannine account and that of the Book of Mormon agree on the presence of the Spirit to aid the participant in the discharge of his covenanted

duties as he obeys the instructions of the Lord.

There are other agreements between the gospel of John and the Book of Mormon account which have no direct bearing on the Lord's Supper and were encountered in the course of the study of Christ's visit to the Americas. Two of them are worth mentioning since they add strength to what has been written:

1. The Book of Mormon does not call the twelve whom Christ chose and ordained on this land "apostles" such as the Synoptics call the twelve in Judea. Similarly, John does not call the twelve chosen and ordained in Judea apostles. As in the Book of Mormon, he calls them disciples.

2. John is the only one of the four evangelists who writes of "other sheep."[57] The Book of Mormon tells us who these other sheep are.[58] (This agreement between the two accounts could be easily dismissed as a missionary device assisting the promulgation of Mormonism. Such is not the case, as will be discovered later in the course of this study, but it is an agreement.)

Summing up the harmonies between the two accounts does not solve the mystery. What puzzles us is the suggestion which comes out of this harmony. This agreement suggests a common source of information available to both John and the writers of the Book of Mormon, yet the two were separated in time and space.

The Book of Mormon tells us that John was known to Nephi through the Spirit.[59] But even when we accept this, how can we trust the account of John when the critics tell us that this gospel was written around A.D. 130-150?

Of special interest to us is the fact that the critics do

not agree on the Greek origin of this gospel. There are some outstanding students who think that John was written by the son of Zebedee in or around Jerusalem and even before the gospel of Mark was written. This is the next topic of discussion.

1. I Nephi 3:165-175.
2. 5:4-19.
3. 5:20-44.
4. 5:45 ff.
5. 6:1-12.
6. 6:13 ff.
7. 7:1-12.
8. 7:13 ff.
9. 8:1-27.
10. 8:28-68.
11. 8:70 ff.
12. 9:39-45.
13. 8:28-31.
14. This quotation from the authorized edition of the Book of Mormon reveals how ill prepared Joseph Smith was academically for the calling which became his. The disproportion between what the Book says and how it is stated is a strong support for its prophetic mission.
15. Williston Walker, *History of Christianity*, Scribner and Sons, p. 56.
16. *Ibid.*, pp. 536-37. (In addition to this see Njeim's "Maturation of My Faith," *Saints' Herald*, Oct. 1, 1968, pp. 21, 26-27.
17. Luke, R.S.V. 22:17-20.
18. Matthew, R.S.V. 26:28; Mark 14:24.
19. James, 14:1-4.
20. *Ibid.*, 19-20.
21. John 14:21.
22. John 14:8, 22.
23. John 13:7.
24. II Nephi 8:39.
25. Moroni 4:4.
26. Acts 2:37 ff.
27. III Nephi 8:40.
28. III Nephi 8:60-62.
29. III Nephi 8:70.
30. III Nephi 9:12-14.
31. Matthew 9:15 (see also Mark 2:18-20).
32. Romans 6:3-11.
33. *Christ the Sacrament of the Encounter with God*, Sheed and Ward,

1963, New York, p. 44.

34. I Corinthians 11:31.
35. I Corinthians 11:16-22.
36. Matthew 16:19; 18:15-18.
37. Mosiah 9:38-42; Alma 5:27.
38. William Barclay, *The Lord's Supper, op. cit.*, p. 107.
39. Moroni, chapters 4 and 5.
40. *The Rise of Christianity, op. cit.*, p. 326.
41. William Barclay, *The Lord's Supper, op. cit.*, p. 63.
42. Moroni 4:4.
43. *Ibid.*, 5:3.
44. *Ibid.*, 4:2-3.
45. *Ibid.*, 2:1.
46. Matthew 6:9-13; Luke 11:2-4.
47. John 17:15-19.
48. Exegesis *Interpreter's Bible*, Vol. 7, p. 308.
49. Evelyn Underhill, *The Mystery of Sacrifice*, Longmans, Green & Co., London, 1948.
50. III Nephi 8:32.
51. John 15:16.
52. John 15:1-8.
53. John 15:7, 10 (also Chapter 14:21-24).
54. John 14:16.
55. John 14:21, 23, 24.
56. Exodus 24:7, 8.
57. John 10:16.
58. III Nephi 7:16-26.
59. I Nephi 3:251.

CHAPTER FOUR

THE AUTHENTICITY OF JOHN'S GOSPEL

It may seem redundant, after the surprising mutual support cited in the preceding chapter between the Johannine account and that of the Book of Mormon, to add a special chapter on the gospel of St. John. This likeness is especially important in view of the fact that, of the four gospels, John's is the only one accredited with apostolic authorship and bearing the name of the author. In addition to this we have the words of the oldest Christian historian, Eusebius, who reports that Clement of Alexandria says of John: "He, being encouraged by his familiar friends, and urged by the Spirit, wrote a spiritual gospel."[1] Also in the chapter, "The order of the Gospels," he mentions that John was the last to write of the ministry of the Lord.[2] R. H. Strachan gives the names of six other writers during the last half of the second century who mention John as the author of this gospel.[3] Yet in spite of all the evidence, this gospel, like the Book of Mormon, is beleagured by the critics, and the credibility of its eyewitness is seriously questioned. Fundamentally at issue is the Christology of the gospel. If it was written by John, the son of

Zebedee, then there is no doubt about the soundness of its claims. But if it was written by someone else and at a much later period in time than previously thought (as some critics assert) then its Christology is a gradual growth which tradition wove around the person of Jesus of Nazareth, thus allowing some to question the historicity of Christ. The debate over this gospel has extended from the middle of the last century to the present. Gradually but surely, however, the early orthodox view of John as author is gaining affirmation, though its advocates are few in number.

What we shall consider here is simply a review of the struggle centering around the main issues of the controversy. This is necessary for a fuller appreciation of the harmony between John and the Book of Mormon.

Higher criticism of this gospel stems from its language, especially that of the prologue—verses 1 through 18. The gospel also differs from the synoptic account in construction and substance. This puts it in a class of its own which generates suspicion in spite of the claims of its eyewitness and what second century writers said of it. The problem is composed of two seemingly linguistic observations which connect it (1) with the Greek Logos and (2) with Gnosticism.

The Logos

The idea of the Logos came to us from the Greeks and was popularlized by the Stoics. In Webster's *Collegiate Dictionary* the term is defined thusly: "The word or form which expresses a thought, also the thought." Then the theological meaning is given and connected with the prologue of this gospel.

The Logos as philosophy spread throughout the Hellenized world of the day. Rabbinic Judaism was isolationist and resisted the introduction of foreign philosophies into its theology. But the Judaism outside Judea was different. Philo of Alexandria translated the Pentateuch into Greek and wrote several treaties on the Old Testament. He used the Logos quite extensively in his writings. To him the Logos was many things, including high priest and the Paraclete—advocate and comforter—the Holy Spirit.[4]

Aside from the first two verses of the first chapter, the fourth gospel is full of Logos thought. In the famous conversation with the Samaritan woman, Jesus referred to himself as the giver of "water springing up into everlasting life."[5] In another passage he was "the bread of life."[6] In a bold declaration at the Feast of Tabernacles he said: "If any man thirst, let him come unto me, and drink."[7] He also promised to send his followers "the Comforter, which is the Holy Ghost."[8] All of this suggested to the early critics a Greek, not a Hebraic origin. In addition, John is mentioned as an "unlearned and ignorant" man[9] which tells against his authorship.

Defenders of the authorship of the son of Zebedee say that it is a mistake to attribute this gospel to anyone other than the apostle John. Jewish literature carried terms similar to the Logos long before the Stoics or Philo used the word. There are four reasons why one should not fall into the temptations of the critics.

1. Because of his unlearned and ignorant state the son of Zebedee could not have imitated Philo or the

Greek writers before him.

2. The Logos to Philo and the Greeks is impersonal and immanent. It is subjective, a property of the mind, an indwelling thought. John's Logos in the fourth gospel is transcendent and incarnate. When he wrote: "The Word was made flesh and lived among us, and we beheld his glory, the glory as of the only begotten of the Father," he was writing of a person, of objective reality manifested in Jesus of Nazareth. His conviction was further supported by the empty tomb and the subsequent appearance of the Lord to the disciples, of whom John was one. Thus the incarnation was not a speculative philosophy devoid of self-existence.

3. The Greek Logos combined "word and reason." The "word" appears frequently in the fourth gospel. At no time does reason appear to be embodied in its language.

4. Logos has been designated as Memra. One should not ignore Edersheim who wrote at the close of the last century. He is quoted by subsequent authors on issues forming the background of the gospels. The Logos is one of them. The word under consideration is the Hebrew "Memra." "Not that the term is exclusively applied to the Divine Logos," says Edersheim. "It stands out as perhaps the most remarkable fact in this literature, that God—not as in His Permanent manifestation, or manifest Presence—but as revealing Himself, is designated Memra."[10] Following this he takes the pains to show how many times the term appears in the many Targums.[11] Then, in a footnote regarding the Targum Onkelos, he refers to a change in Deuteronomy 33:27. Instead of "underneath are the

everlasting arms," he has: "And by His Memra was the world created." This is exactly like John 1:10. Thus it is seen that before the Platonic and Stoical Logos, the Hebrews wrote in their differing translations of the Old Testament that God is a revealing God, and this revelation is best manifested in Jesus the Messiah. The Greeks had an idea, but the Jews had a person in mind. For this reason modern commentators and critics write very little if any about the Philo Logos. The best example of this is the introduction to John's Gospel in the *Interpreter's Bible*. The Logos is hardly mentioned, and when it is, the author attributes it to previous Jewish sources.

Gnosticism

Gnosticism was a religious and philosophical movement which gathered into its belief elements from Babylonian, Persian, Egyptian, and Greek thought. It is much older than Christianity but influenced the church considerably. Its best age of development was around the middle of the second century. Its main concern was with redemption.

The world according to the Gnostics was created by two gods. One was the good god associated with light. The other was an inferior god, the creator of this material world, associated with darkness. Hence all matter was regarded by Gnostics as evil. They believed that in order to escape from this evil world one had to have knowledge (gnosis) to reach immortality or the god of light. Only some could attain this high state; others would be lost. Later, after its contact with Christianity, an intermediate physical state was conceived as being attainable. The initiate had to go through mystical ceremonies and sacraments to learn the password. This was necessary in order to get by the seven astral angels (planets) and reach the world of light. Consequently the good was contrasted with evil and light with darkness.

As it came in contact with Christianity the "gnosis" became "revelation." In addition, it went by the name "Christian." To some of its thinkers, the God of the Old Testament was an inferior god. The good god was Christ. For this reason they attempted to divorce Christ from any connection with the Old Testament. To accomplish this they revised the gospels and wrote new ones. One, Marcion, appears to have spearheaded this movement. Since flesh was evil, Christ to them did not appear in the flesh. The eye simply saw an apparent body, a ghost. The crucifixion, resurrection, and ascension were figments of the imagination.

There are those who attribute the Christian origin of Gnosticism to Simon Magus,[12] but the premise lacks certainty. Because of its synchronistic nature they have difficulty arriving at its Christian beginning. There appears to be agreement, however, that during the second quarter of the first half of the second century it emerged as a Christian philosophy with differing branches. The segment with which we are concerned is called "Docetism."

Thus the twin questions of the Logos and literature of the Gnostics fired the imagination of the critics who challenged the traditional view of John's Gospel. Whoever authored it, they argued, wrote to refute the claims of the Gnostics. Since these people denied that Jesus had flesh and blood, the author of the fourth gospel took an opposite view to an established issue.

Jesus was not a ghost. The "word was made flesh, and dwelt among us, and we beheld his glory." The author repeats this in 6:51, 54, and 55. He even makes the audience exclaim: "How can this man give us his flesh to eat?" The Gnostics contrasted light with darkness; the author of this document does the same, but connects the light with the person of Jesus. It was "obvious" to the critics that the writer of John was acquainted with Gnostic literature and was rebutting it. Also, since their claims and literature did not appear until years after the son of Zebedee was dead, the author must be another John, or perhaps one writing in the name of John but not the apostle. Eusebius, as we have already seen, fixes the date of serious Gnostic claims to the years 117 to 138. This helped the critics assign the time of writing of the fourth gospel to the second half of the second century. Some even went further to the extreme and thought the last period of the century was more accurate.

Apostle John as the Author

The critics' argument in favor of authorship other than that of the apostle is not solid. It rests on the assumption that this gospel was written to refute Gnostic heresies. Yet forty to fifty years before it was written, and before Gnosticism was known to the Church, Paul wrote: "Though we have known Christ after the flesh, yet now henceforth, know we him no more."[13] Again on another occasion he wrote: "God was manifest in the flesh, justified in the Spirit, seen of angels, preached unto the Gentiles, believed on in the world, received up into glory."[14] These declarations are simply statements of fact and not an answer to phantom antagonists. Likewise, John's references to the flesh are statements of fact and preceded the appearance of Gnosticism.

The critics also depend on the embellished evidence that the name "Apostle John" as author does not appear in the book. There is an unnamed disciple who might be the author and it would be wrong, they claim, to say this unnamed writer is John. True, but the attribution to the son of Zebedee rests on good authority—transmitted apostolic authority. Irenaeus knew Polycarp personally and heard his discourses. To Florinus he wrote: "I can tell also the very place where the blessed Polycarp was accustomed to sit and discourse," and tell of his "familiar intercourse with John."[15] Irenaeus also wrote: "Afterwards John, the disciple of our Lord, the same that lay upon his bosom, also published the Gospel, whilest he was yet at Ephesus."[16] In addition to these the testimonies of Clement[17] and of Origen[18] confirm the statements of Irenaeus.

Thus when Irenaeus identified John as "the disciple of our Lord, the same that lay upon his bosom," he identified the son of Zebedee. The only disciple that leaned on Jesus' bosom is mentioned in the account of the Lord's Supper,[19] and later on in the conversation between Peter and the Lord.[20] Though the name is not mentioned, it leaves no doubt that he was the apostle John and the one who "wrote these things."

Irenaeus' testimony, solid as it is, is hardly something to cheer about. The critics say that he quotes from Papias that he (Papias) "was John's hearer and the associate of Polycarp." Yet in the same reference

Papias states that his information came from the elders, and since there were two Johns in Ephesus—John the Apostle and John the Presbyter—the gospel could be attributed to the second one.[21]

Witness of the Record

When this gospel account is considered, the evidence points to the apostle as its author. The "we" in verse 14 of the prologue refers to a group of witnesses who "beheld his glory." Since the Lord made his physical appearance to the eleven disciples, the writer must have been of them.

In the final chapter of the gospel the risen Lord appears to seven of his disciples (verse 2). Among them is the disciple "whom Jesus loved" (verse 7). The disciple is further identified as the one who "leaned on" Jesus' "breast at supper" (verse 20), which refers back to the eucharistic meal.[22] It is the same disciple who "testifieth of these things, and wrote these things" (verse 24). The name of the disciple is not given, but it says that he authored this gospel.

In the midst of his agony on the cross, Jesus saw his mother and the disciple "whom he loved." Simultaneously he entrusted his mother to the care of this disciple. The man took her to his home.[23] The significance of this statement lies in the fact that while the other disciples fled,[24] this one remained and witnessed the crucifixion. He tells us in clear words that the soldiers did not break Jesus' legs, because he was already dead, and saw that one of them took a spear and pierced his sides from whence issued blood mixed with water. "And he that saw it bear record, and his record is true: and he knoweth that he saith true, that ye might believe."[25]

Why did this disciple stay and witness the final suffering of Jesus while the others fled? He was acquainted with the high priest and did not fear being implicated. He and Peter followed Jesus to the high priest's palace, which he entered—but Peter did not. Because of this acquaintance he was able to secure permission for Peter to enter the hall of trial.[26]

This is a gospel of intimacy. There is careful precision of details regarding individuals and circumstances. The writer had intimate, not transmitted knowledge. The only members of the Twelve who qualified for this intimacy were Peter, James, and John. Jesus chose them to be with him on the mount of transfiguration and to be close to him in the agonizing vigil before his death.[27] Peter was out of the picture as the author. James was already dead. Thus the writer would seem to be the apostle John, the beloved disciple who "leaned on Jesus' breast" during the Eucharist, who adopted Mary the mother of Jesus, and who was a witness to the crucifixion. This high probability gains credence with Paul's calling James, Cephas, and John as pillars in the church.[28] Because of the detailed nature of this gospel, it must have been written by a leader who had a prominent position in the movement. The focus rests on John.

Defenders of apostolic authorship, after further examination of the record, uncovered additional support. These studies yielded astonishing results. It was discovered that the writer was well acquainted with the Old Testament and referred to it frequently without giving the exact quote.[29] He was also acquainted with the geography of the country and knew the topography of the land. He distinguished between the two Bethanies.[30] Aenon was near Salem,[31] and Ephraim was by the wilderness.[32] Sychar was close to the parcel of land Jacob gave to Joseph.[33] He knew Jerusalem and its surroundings.[34] The pavement in the palace had another name and so did Golgotha.[35] He knew the exact time[36] and even mentioned the hour of the day. In addition to this he recorded exact numbers.[37] He was a contemporary of events and individuals.[38] For these reasons, he had to be the son of Zebedee.

To further support the traditional claims of this gospel, Torrey translated it from Greek into the Aramaic of Palestine in order to remove the hesitance over some of its wording which did not appear to be Greek and confused the issue.[39] The attempt was made to prove that the author was a Jew who wrote in the language of the time.

In another book Torrey says: "The work of the Fourth Evangelist seems to be distinctly a Jerusalem Gospel; written by one who was especially interested in that city or probably resided there."[40] When it comes to the dating of this gospel he does not hesitate to say that it was written prior to the year A.D. 70. He depends on what he calls the "argument of silence." None of the four gospels mentions "the destruction of the temple or the devastation of Jerusalem by the Romans under Titus. . . . There is no evidence whatever tending to show that any one of the writers whose work appears in these documents had knowledge of the terrible, epoch-making catastrophe of the year 70 such as Josephus describes."[41] Thus Torrey appears to be in the vanguard of a few influential students who attribute the fourth gospel to John and fix its date prior to A.D. 70.

The Critics' Rebuttal

The critics agree with the conclusion that a Jew of Palestine was the author but reject the idea that it was written prior to A.D. 70 and that John was the author. Two reasons support them in their stand. The first is the conflict between Irenaeus and Papias over the two Johns which has already been discussed. The second is the late appearance of the gospel. What bothers the critics is the absence of any reference to the gospel and its author by the fathers who wrote during the first half of the second century. Ignatius, Bishop of Antioch and second in apostolic succession, does not mention it; neither does Papias, Bishop of Hierapolis and a contemporary of Polycarp. All the writers who support apostolic authorship belong to the second half of the century. Justin Martyr mentions the gospel but his dependence is mainly on the synoptic record. Consequently, the issue remains unresolved.

Archaeological Support

New Testament archaeology is recent, and because the Christian Church found its development outside Palestine, Palestinian discoveries relative to the beginning of Christianity are few—but significant. Archaeology has shed some light on the fourth gospel and does help in the clarification of the cloudy issues which the internal evidence does not solve. Thus the emerging archaeological story deserves detailed attention. It contributes to the solution of the

109

Gnostic problem and shortens the gap between the proponents and opponents of apostolic authorship.

It appears from recent archaeological finds that the claims of early critics that this gospel was written in answer to Gnostic beliefs are now considerably weakened. J. A. Thompson, who has done archaeological work in Palestine, has this to say on the subject:

> Up to recent times our knowledge of the Gnostics had come at second hand, largely from the church Fathers. Whereas we had only three original codices and seven different writings a few years ago, we now have thirteen codices and forty-four different writings. Of all the various Gnostic works mentioned by the Fathers, only a few are now missing. It becomes clear that the picture drawn by the Fathers was a true one. Indeed, on the evidence of the new material, the early Gnostics were even worse heretics than the Fathers indicated. The supposed form of mild Gnosticism that is said to have influenced John was simply non-existent in the second century when the Gospel of John was supposed to have been written, and when John supposedly came under their influence.[42]

Following this Thompson discusses the Qumran material which embodies a dualism similar to that of the Gnostics. This community's dualism may have had its origin by contact with Persian thought. But under the influence of Jewish teachings it had become thoroughly Judaized. Both evil and good were created by God. Man had the right of choice. In support of this view he quotes Albright as follows:

> This simple dualism, contrasting good and evil, truth and falsehood, light and darkness, appears in the Gospel of John; there is nothing Gnostic about it, and those many N. T. scholars who date the Gospel after the rise of Gnosticism are now proved wrong. The Gospel of John is saturated with phraseology and conceptual imagery reminding us of the Dead Sea Scrolls.[43]

I find Albright's work exciting though not conclusive. His findings do not support the belief that the Gospels were originally written in Aramaic; instead, Aramaic was the oral language of these documents before they were written in Greek. Some students who might still attribute such words as rabbi, Rabboni, master (John 1:38; 20:16)—which in Greek are rendered *Didaskalos*—as being borrowed from second century usage when the word was used in the Mishnah and other writings of the period, are bound to be disappointed.

Albright writes:

> In 1930 E. L. Sukenik excavated a tomb in the property of the Hebrew University on Mount Scopus, and discovered in it an ossuary on which was the Greek name Theodotion in Aramaic characters, as well as the Greek word "didaskalos" as title of the man who bore this name. Henceforth it cannot be safely alleged that the Gospel of John is anachronistic in this particular respect.[44]

To others who thought that personal names in this gospel were fictitious, more ossuary inscriptions proved them wrong. He states:

> The ossuary inscriptions disprove such speculations by preserving many of these very same names (Pl. 30). Thus we find commonly on them, not only Miriam (Mary), but also Martha, Elizabeth, Salome, Johnna, etc. The name Sapphira (Acts 5:1) also appears repeatedly. Jesus (Jeshua) and Joseph are, of course, among the commonest names of the period, and an ossuary containing the name of a Jesus, son of Joseph, though exciting surprise at first, reflects one of the most ordinary combinations of the time.[45]

The Earliest Gospel Papyrus

The moving factor behind the return to the proximity of the orthodox view of this gospel, such as Torrey and others present, is the discovery in a small town in Egypt of the oldest gospel fragment. It has the distinction of belonging to John's Gospel. (The translation took place in 1935.) Of it Thompson writes:

111

It was a small piece of papyrus only three and a half by two and a half inches, containing fragments of John's Gospel, chapter 18, verses 31 to 33 and 37 and 38. The style of writing enabled it to be assigned to the first half of the second century. As we have seen, the fact that it was not only written in Egypt but that it had been used in a provincial town in Egypt at this early date points to the fact that John's Gospel, far from being a late second century production as some maintained, was in fact far earlier, and more likely to have been written in the first century, or at least very early in the second. Up the present this is our earliest piece of the New Testament.[46]

Albright, who wrote earlier than Thompson, had arrived at the same conclusion. He dates the origin of this gospel at between A.D. 80 and 90.[47] Indeed he mentions other students who date its writing earlier than this, and one who thinks this gospel was written before the synoptics.[48]

Summary of the Critical Problem

It is clear from this all-too-short review that there is no consensus among students on the author of this gospel, and neither is there agreement on the date when it was written. All one can say is that the Gnostic issue and the Greek Logos idea attributed to this document are now remote if not dead issues. The main concern is the historicity of the gospel and the person it depicts. Is this gospel forged, and is the person it portrays fictitious? Or is it authentic and the historical Jesus a real figure? In view of what has been written on the subject in little more than a hundred years of debate, the investigator is no wiser now than he was before. The papyrus discovery puts the gospel at an earlier date than previously determined, but the question remains: Why was it not mentioned prior to the second half of the second century?

Dodd, perhaps, gave the best summary when he wrote: "The long debate has so far been inconclusive, and is perhaps likely to remain so, until some happy accident should bring us altogether fresh evidence."[49]

The Divine Design

"Accidents" have added immeasurably to the clarification of the sacred word. The Egyptian papyrus and the Dead Sea Scroll discoveries came about by accident. Dodd's hope for another accident is sound, but Christianity is the result of a divine design, not an accident. Since this is the case, we must look to the Author of our faith to rescue his gospel from the critics. Fortunately, the coming forth of the Book of Mormon was part of this divine design.

Of the twelve apostles the Lord had in Judea, John has the distinction of being the only one mentioned by name and titled "the apostle of the lamb" in the Book of Mormon. A casual reading of the account which refers to him prompts us to dismiss it as contrary to common sense. But with study and perseverance we find its divine credentials coming to the surface.[50] The statement connects John with the apocalypse and not with this gospel. Since John was to write, however, the probability exists that he was intended also to write the gospel bearing his name. Support for this probability was revealed in our investigation of the Lord's Supper. The agreement on so many of the baffling issues of the Eucharist between the fourth gospel and the Book of Mormon are interesting, to say the least. There are three possibilities which may explain this harmony. The first is that the account of the Book of Mormon was humanly contrived to make it agree with the fourth gospel. The second is that the Book of Mormon account accidentally happened to agree with John's account. And the third is that it was divinely designed that the Book of Mormon support John's account on the subject. If the last one is chosen—and I can find no rationale which supports the first two possibilities—then the fourth gospel emerges as the production of the son of Zebedee.

For a direct statement referring to John as the author of this gospel, we cannot ignore the introduction to Section 7 of the Doctrine and Covenants. This was given through the Urim and Thummim and stands on the same level of authority as the Book of Mormon. It appears that a discussion arose between Joseph Smith and Oliver Cowdery concerning the word "tarry" in John 21:21-24. The information they received was "translated from parchment, written and hid up by himself [John]." Since this involves the bewildering problem of these four verses, we have every reason to believe that the whole gospel was written early by the apostle and sealed up until after his death. For those who may draw a conclusion from this revelation and think John is still living in a mortal state such as we are, acquaintance with his concept of life and death may help (John 11:25, 26).

This action should not be considered a strange procedure. Jewish hostility to the claims of Jesus was bitter and strong and did not cease after his death. The authorities bribed the guards at the tomb, asking them to say: "His disciples came by night, and stole him away while we slept."[51] Stephen was stoned to death for his bold and uncompromising testimony.[52] The apostle James, brother of John, was beheaded,[53]

114

and Peter was thrown into jail. Even away from Jerusalem, life for a witness of Christ was not safe. Paul had to flee from Damascus or be killed.[54] He did not find safety even when he went back to Jerusalem. There were plots on his life, and the Saints had to smuggle him out of the city to the nearest seaport and ship him to Tarsus.[55] The Jews stalked him from city to city. Had it not been for divine help and the Roman authorities he would have been killed.[56] Only Roman interference saved him from death at the hands of disorderly mobs when he returned to Jerusalem for the second time and was finally sent as a prisoner to Rome.[57] Frustrated at the escape of their prey, the mob turned and killed the brother of the Lord, James the Just. He was thrown from the wing of the temple and clubbed to death.[58] In an atmosphere like this, John must have considered that the hand of the assassin would soon reach him. Nothing could have been more natural for the remaining free "pillar" of the infant church than to write an eyewitness history of the brief ministry of Jesus for the benefit of future generations.

Fortunately, we now have parallels for the action taken by John. In an atmosphere such as has been described, claims and counterclaims have the tendency to multiply and radically distort the truth. John may have heard many of these distortions as the story of Jesus was told and retold. In order to set the record straight he wrote what he did and kept it hidden until tempers were calmed and the danger was past. The Dead Sea Scrolls were hidden to preserve the truth and keep the word from falling into the hands of the enemy. Modern governments do the same in times of hostility and extreme danger to the state. Important documents are hidden so the orderly function of government may be restored when peace is secured. John's writing and protecting the fourth gospel should not be considered a unique act; under the circumstances, it was quite proper.

This safekeeping of the gospel also accounts for its late appearance. John died in Ephesus at a ripe old age. It is reasonable to assume that his story of Jesus was securely left with a trusted friend to be published after his death. Polycarp is the friend suggested. It is significant that Irenaeus does not say that the gospel was written at Ephesus. It was "published" or "circulated" at Ephesus.

John's Motive Clarified

Another factor supporting the early authorship of the gospel may be adduced from the book of Revelation. Ancient Christian fathers attribute both documents to the son of Zebedee. It is also agreed by most authorities that Revelation was written around A.D. 96-97 and was in circulation shortly afterward. Its message carries clear evidence of strong Roman persecution of the infant church. Its apocalyptic language is intended to shield the author and the church from retribution, yet give prophetic reason for resistance. The fourth gospel contains no hint of persecution. This forces us to the belief that it was written before any persecution of the church ever took place, including the Nero atrocities and the destruction of Jerusalem. Also, the fact that it is written in plain language (in opposition to Revelation) is a good reason why the author withheld it from circulation. This gospel appears to be anti-Jewish,[59] and its publication would inflame animosity toward the leaders of the church. Roman brutalities simply added to the necessity for precaution. Considering the precarious Jewish national situation around the advent of the Lord and the difficult circumstances surrounding the emerging church, John's withholding of this historic document was most prudent.

The Mutuality Factor

The main evidence, however, for the authenticity of this gospel is found in the unanticipated harmony its account of the Lord's Supper has with the Book of Mormon. The introduction of the statement from the Doctrine and Covenants is only supportive. It gives a clue for the late appearance of the gospel. But the harmony found in the previous chapters is the key to the solution of the puzzle which eluded the critics. It is in the rejection of the Passover issue by John and the silence of the Book of Mormon on the same that the authorship of John is confirmed. The agreement of both on the requirement for priestly authority in the administration of this sacrament cannot be ignored. Also, with the discovery of the lost prayer the Lord pronounced in consecrating the emblems, and its harmony with the consecration prayer of the Twelve in Palestine, the authorship of John, the son of Zebedee, is difficult to resist.

Left alone, the Gospel of John will always be under suspicion. The same is true of the Book of Mormon. Once their testimony is combined, however, their authority is respected.

Authority of the Word

What John is trying to convey to the reader in his gospel is the primary importance of *the word* to Jesus, whether that word is capitalized (as is the case in the prologue) or in small letters (as it is found in the rest of this document). "In the beginning was the Word, and the Word was with God, and the Word was God." This "Word was made flesh and dwelt among us." The word—small letter—is spirit (6:63). The word will judge humanity (12:47, 48). Obedience to the word means love for Christ; treating it lightly means the opposite (14:23). The word is not Christ's; it belongs to the One who sent him (14, 24). When the word is strictly observed it cleanses (15:3); it also gives security (15:7).

The most striking feature which stands out in this gospel is the insistence of Jesus on the word when he was facing Calvary and the cross. The occasion was the conclusion of the Lord's Supper when his severest trial was about to begin. He concluded the festivity with a prayer.[60] There appeared in it no concern whatsoever about what was to happen to him. His only concern was with the word. First, he asked that he might glorify the Father (verse 1). Then he gave thanks to the Father for the gift of the twelve. He gave them the words the Father gave him (verse 8), and they kept them (verse 6). Because of the word, the world "hath hated them" (verse 14), but he did not ask for them to be taken out of this world (verse 15). His petition was that they might be sanctified "through thy truth; thy word is truth" (verse 17). The reason for this request was that they (the twelve) were being sent "into the world," as he was sent. The most striking petition, however, came at the conclusion of the prayer. He still showed no sign of concern over his impending tragic death. Instead, his concern was over future generations and their attitude toward the word. "Neither pray I for these alone, but for them also which shall believe on me through their word" (verse 20).

The emphasis on the word and the sanctification for it is a singular feature of this gospel and the eucharistic prayer Jesus pronounced on the elements on this hemisphere. In the synoptic account, Jesus put emphasis on his words, sayings, and doctrines. But the difference here lies in the fact that the setting, wording, and substance which John reported have their sequel only in the American Eucharist. In both the setting was the Lord's Supper. The wording of sanctification appears in both. Yet, while in John the emphasis is on the word, the emphasis in the Lord's eucharistic prayer is on the commandment—same substance. Another noticeable feature of John's account was the lengthy Lord's Supper exhortation Jesus gave to the twelve before they were consecrated, namely, the promise of the presence of the Spirit in them if they kept his words (14:16, 17, 26, 27; 15:13). The surprising thing is that this promise has its counterpart only in the Lord's Supper prayer pronounced on this hemisphere.

Another distinctive feature is that at both occasions and settings, preeminence was given to the word first and then to the Spirit. This was not accidental. It was a fundamental order. Its reversal led the Christian church into divisive theological controversies and in extreme cases into antinomianism.[61] The church fell victim to this reversal at Nauvoo when the word was clear on marriage. As the Spirit took precedence over the word, the church suffered and strange theological innovations had to be found to justify the ugly deed.

Warning in this regard was given to the church as early as 1832 when the Lord said that "condemnation" rested on the church if "the new covenant, even the Book of Mormon" was ignored. We in the Reorganization are suffering from this condemnation because we have neglected the book. Happily, however, the promise of acceptance is given on the ground of repentance.[62]

It is hoped that now, since the critical clouds are lifted from both the gospel according to John and the Lord's Supper as mentioned in the Book of Mormon, their authority will become binding on us. The means for accomplishing this renewal is the sacrament of the Lord's Supper. It is here that we are reminded of the commandments, as far as the Book of Mormon is concerned, and the words as stated in the eucharistic instruction by John. This may mean that we shall suffer for the word as the apostolic church did, but we also have the comforting promise of the Holy Spirit.

1. *Eusebius Ecclesiastical History*, Book VI, Chapter 14.
2. *Ibid.*, Book III, Chapter 24.
3. *Dictionary of Christ and the Gospels*, John, Gospel of.
4. Edersheim, *Life and Times of Jesus the Messiah*, Vol. 1, p. 49, Longmans, 1898.
5. John 4:16.
6. John 6:48.
7. John 7:37.
8. John 14:26.
9. Acts 4:13.

10. Edersheim, *op. cit.*, Vol. 1, pp. 46-47.
11. Targum is a translation of the Old Testament into the Aramaic of Palestine.
12. *Ecclesiastical History*, Book IV, Chapter 7.
13. II Corinthians 5:16, K.J.
14. I Timothy 3:16.
15. *Ecclesiastical History*, Book V, Chapter 20.
16. *Ibid.*, Book V, Chapter 8.
17. *Ibid.*, Book III, Chapter 23.
18. *Ibid.*, Book VI, Chapter 25.
19. John 13:23.
20. John 21:20.
21. *Ecclesiastical History*, Book III, Chapter 39.
22. John 13:23-35.
23. John 19:25-27.
24. Matthew 26:56, Mark 14:50.
25. John 19:33-35.
26. John 18:15-16.
27. Matthew 17:1; 26:37; Mark 5:37.
28. Galatians 2:9.
29. 12:38; 13:18; 17:12; 19:24, 28, 36, 37.
30. 1:28; 11:18.
31. 3:23.
32. 11:54.
33. 4:5.
34. 5:2; 18:1.
35. 19:13, 17.
36. 1:29; 2:1; 4:40; 6:22; 7:14; 11:6; 12:1; 19:31; 20:1. The hour: 1:39; 4:6; 19:14.
37. 1:35; 2:6; 6:9, 10, 19; 4:18; 19:23, 39.
38. For additional details see "Gospel of John," by R. H. Strachan in *Dictionary of Christ and the Gospels.*
39. Charles Cutler Torrey, *The Four Gospels*, Harper Brothers.
40. Charles Cutler Torrey, *The Origin of the Gospels*, p. 263.
41. *Ibid.*, pp. 155-157.
42. J. A. Thompson, *Archaeology, Archaeology of the New Testament,* Eerdman's, 1959, p. 117.
43. *Ibid.*, p. 118.
44. W. F. Albright, *The Archaeology of Palestine*, 1954, p. 244.
45. Albright, *The Archaeology of Palestine*, *op. cit.*, pp. 138-139.
46. Thompson, *Archaeology of the New Testament*, *op. cit.*, pp. 138-139.
47. Albright, *The Archaeology of Palestine*, *op cit.*, p. 244.
48. *Ibid.*, p. 240.
49. C. H. Dodd, *Historical Tradition in the Fourth Gospel*, Cambridge University Press, 1965.
50. See my book, *Insights into the Book of Revelation*, 1970.
51. Matthew 28:11-15.
52. Acts 7:54 ff.

53. Acts 12:2, 3.
54. Acts 9:23-25.
55. Acts 9:26-30.
56. Acts 17:5-10; 18:12-16.
57. Acts 21-26.
58. *Ecclesiastical History*, Book II, Chapter 23.
59. Samuel Sandmel, *A Jewish Understanding of the New Testament*, Hebrew Union College Press, 1957, p. 269.
60. John 17.
61. See my publication *Insights into the Book of Revelation*, pp. 34-37.
62. Doctrine and Covenants 83:8.

CHAPTER FIVE

RELATIONSHIP OF BAPTISM TO THE LORD'S SUPPER

Latter Day Saints have a distinctive vocabulary connected with baptism and the Lord's Supper. To those not affiliated with the church, this language may sound like a departure from the ordinary Christian norm—perhaps even a bit heretical. Similar to other Christian sects, Saints believe that baptism is necessary for the remission of sins. But quite often when this sacrament is administered it is referred to as a "covenant." The Lord's Supper to the average Christian is a "covenant"; but among Saints, partaking of the sacred meal is referred to as a "renewal of the covenant." This change in language was influenced by the Book of Mormon account. When the sacrament of baptism was first instituted on this hemisphere (before the visit of Christ) it was called a covenant.[1] This, as stated by Yale and Brockway,[2] leaves no doubt. There is, however, no reason given for this change. It is taken on faith.

The premise here is clear. Once baptism is established as a covenant, it then follows that the Lord's Supper is a renewal of this covenant. The challenge now is to find a historical and biblical basis for this concept.

Origin of Religious Covenants

The first religious covenant of any lasting significance

had its origin in the encounter of Abraham with God.[3] For this reason the impact of the covenant on the religious life of Israel was momentous. In the course of time it influenced the adoption of baptism. Each item of Abraham's covenant is pregnant with meaning and becomes fundamental to our study.

The tendency is to begin analysis with Abraham as the first principal of the covenant. This is wrong. The story starts with God as the prime mover. Abraham, whose name was still Abram, was lost as to the meaning of life. At ninety and nine years of age he still had no male heir—the one blessing deeply cherished by the people of that period. It was not the natural thing for a man as old as Abraham to father children. Whether he was in the midst of despair or hope is not known. This much we know, however: God took the initiative. In introducing himself, he addressed Abram with, "I am the Almighty God." This signified a distinction between the gods fashioned by men of that day, whose power was nil, and the God who created humanity. Following this introduction, the Almighty One proposed a covenant. He would give Abram a son as well as the land of Canaan in which he was then sojourning. The divine pledge, however, was not unconditional. Abram was to "walk before me, and be thou perfect." At this point Abram's name was changed to Abraham, whose silence indicated his acceptance of the offer. Every pledge required a sign of consent, and the one proposed here was the circumcision of the foreskin of every male descendant. It included "every man child in your generations." And not only they, but every male "that is born in thy house, and he that is bought with thy money, must needs be circumcised."[4] Hence the descendants of

124

Abraham and his acquired servants were bound by this covenant.

Walking before God and being perfect is not an easy task as one may suppose. It meant that, as God revealed his will to Abraham and generations after him, they were duty-bound to obey that will or suffer the consequences. Abraham himself became an example of obedience to the revealed will of God. When his only son, Isaac, was required by the Lord for sacrifice, Abraham obeyed, painful though that decision must have been.[5] It is for this reason that he is called the father of the faithful by Jews, Moslems, and Christians.

Adverse examples of those who take this covenant lightly are found on many of the pages of the Old Testament. Outstanding among prophetic pronouncements was Jeremiah's warning. "Obey my voice, and I will be your God, and ye shall be my people; and walk ye in all the ways I have commanded you, that it may be well unto you. But they hearkened not, nor inclined their ear, but walked in the counsel and in the imagination of their evil heart, and went backward and not forward."[6] The result of this backsliding was the captivity in Babylon. Circumcision alone without keeping the words of the Lord did not make for a covenant.

It could be rightly argued that circumcision was practiced by other people. This is true, but it was not a sign of a covenant to them. The ancient Arabs and Egyptians practiced it for hygienic and tribal-marking purposes. The Aztecs and other Central American tribes practiced the ritual as well, but it remained for the Almighty God to take a common practice and make it the symbol of a covenant.[7]

The Covenant and Proselytes

The Hebrews are not a homogeneous people. As Abraham journeyed from one settlement to another, he acquired friends and servants who desired to go with him on his travels. According to Jewish commentators, those who made the choice became proselytes and in time were regarded as Hebrews. The means of initiation included baptism.[8]

There were several types of proselytes, but the ones we are concerned with were called "proselytes of righteousness." Three things were required of them if they were to become "children of the covenant and perfect Israelites": circumcision, baptism, and sacrifice.[9] In the case of the women, baptism and Qorban were sufficient. Edersheim[10] adds: "That *baptism* was absolutely necessary to make a proselyte is so frequently stated as not to be disputed." Before this inquiry is closed, a word on the mode of their baptism is enlightening. "The person to be baptized, having cut his hair and nails, undressed completely, made fresh profession of his faith before what were designated 'the fathers of baptism' . . . and then immersed completely, so that every part of the body was touched by the water."[11] Apparently the individual immersed himself. Thus the introduction of baptism to proselytes took the place of ancient circumcision among the descendants of Abraham. This change did not happen suddenly and without dispute. One school of thought required baptism without circumcision, while the other required circumcision without baptism. Finally the debate was settled by requiring both. At what point in history this took place Edersheim does not exactly say. But Moore, who wrote later, supported Edersheim's observation, adding: "The

origin of the requirement of baptism is not known."[12]
Oesterley, however, in his article on circumcision says:

Whatever may have been the original object and signification of circumcision, it had lost its primary meaning long before the time of our Lord. ...In latter days there arose a divergence of opinion among the Jews as to the need of circumcision for proselytes ...affirming that baptism was sufficient.

Then he adds an important conclusion: "...in the opinion of a very influential and important class of Jews, circumcision and baptism were analogous rites."[13]

The Baptism of John

This background sets the stage for the mission of John. He was singularly different from Jewish theologians, however. Whereas they argued and reasoned out the requirements of the law for the admission of proselytes to the covenant of Israel, John was a prophet with a message to Israel itself. The kingdom of heaven was at hand, but the Israelites were spiritually and morally unprepared for its reception. They needed to repent and be baptized, as proselytes were, to be worthy of citizenship in the "Rule of God." It was this insistence on baptism which gave John the nickname of "Baptist."

The story of John is simply and briefly told in the New Testament. But behind this simplicity and brevity lies an important and far-reaching message which has a very significant bearing on us today. The limited account is best found in Matthew and Luke.[14] We would like to have more details of the encounter of this prophet with the Jews, but the record does not provide it. Two major concerns arise from the account we have, however. Why such an exodus of people to his baptism, and why the denunciation of the Pharisees and Sadducees? Other questions arising from these two will be answered

127

in the course of the investigation.

The first eye-catching feature of this story is the way the Jews responded to John's preaching. The people of "Jerusalem, and all Judea, and all the region round about Jordan . . . were baptized of him in Jordan, confessing their sins."[15] By any account this is a sizable number. It does not mean that everyone in these places was baptized, but it does mean that a great majority were. Why?

In a very cryptic way John gives the answer in the following verse: "O generation of vipers, who hath warned you to flee from the wrath to come?" These people were running away from danger, and the danger was implied from John's message: "The kingdom of heaven is at hand." But the people were not ready to receive it; they were unclean. The cry was: "Prepare ye the way of the Lord, make his paths straight."

This may sound meaningless to us, but to the Jews the message was crystal clear. First, they were governed by a ruthless foreign power out of whose clutches there was no apparent way of escape. Roman law and Jewish law were antithetical—the one was human, the other divine. There was no possible way of reconciling them. Already significant hostility between the two was emerging.[16] In this atmosphere the Jews turned to the only thing they knew—the law and the prophets. But more than that there was a living prophet in their midst. They had already heard him quote Isaiah and undoubtedly other prophecies pointing to the coming of the Messiah and the relief he would bring. One of those who had heard John preach about the coming kingdom was Andrew, Simon Peter's brother. He went out and told others who were searching. They rejoiced because they had "found the Messias, which is, being interpreted, the Christ." The same joy was experienced by Philip and Nathanael.[17] Here was the answer to freedom from Rome. Purification through baptism made them ready for the new king.

Next, they went to John and the river Jordan to confess their sins and be baptized. What was there in the waters of the river that would protect them from the wrath that was coming? This is the question in the minds of many who read the account. It bothered the Pharisees and the Sadducees of that day but from a different perspective than it perplexes people now; but to those who were brave enough to confess their sins there was no problem. They were defiled and, as the law prescribed, they were washing away their sins. They were estranged from the covenant of God and, like proselytes, they were making a new covenant. This was not simply a ceremonial washing. They were morally and spiritually committing themselves—first to God, and then to the keeping of his instructions. No kingdom could be built without this dual pledge, and they understood it.

The Pharisees and Sadducees presented another problem. If they were convinced of John's prophetic mission, they certainly had reservations about his baptism. Could they—who were already Jews of the blood line of Abraham, circumcised when eight days old—accept the humiliation of being counted as gentiles and submit to baptism? Edersheim puts their problem this way:

> Was it intended, that the hearers of John should give this as evidence of their repentance, that, like persons defiled, they sought purification, and, like strangers, they sought admission among the people who took on themselves the Rule of God?[18]

Their hesitancy or doubt may be traced to their false pride. Although the text does not say it in so many words, John knew what was going on in their minds. That is why he said to them: "And think not to say within yourselves, We have Abraham to our father: for I say unto you, that God is able of these stones to raise up children unto Abraham."[19] God made a covenant with Abraham, and Abraham kept it by walking before him and being perfect in obedience to his will. They simply had the sign of the covenant in their circumcision, walked in their way, and trusted in the Abrahamic merit.

Behind them there was also a tradition which was difficult to overcome. Again, Edersheim writes:

In fact, by their descent from Abraham, all the children of Israel were nobles, infinitely higher than any proselytes. What, exclaims the Talmud, "shall the born Israelite stand upon the earth, and the proselyte be in heaven?" In fact, the ships on the sea were preserved through the merit of Abraham; the rain descended on account of it. For his sake alone had Moses been allowed to ascend into heaven, and to receive the law; for his sake the sin of the golden calf had been forgiven; his righteousness had on many occasion been the support of Israel's cause.

Then he quotes the Midrash: "If thy children [Abraham's] were even [morally] dead bodies, without blood vessels or bones, thy merit would avail for them!"[20] With such beliefs, the Pharisees and Sadducees had difficulty consenting to John's baptism.

Objections Raised

It was only natural that as the discovery of a Jewish background for baptism was developed during the last part of the nineteenth century objections to it developed also. It came from Calvinists, Lutherans, and Baptists. Their assumption was based on the New Testament account, namely, that baptism had its origin with the

130

prophetic mission of John. It was disquieting to discover the opposite. The debate has died down, and the majority of students believe now in its antiquity. A few, like Berkouwer, still see some difference between the two baptisms, but their objections are tempered by the continuing evidence. "But this baptism," he writes, "did not serve to make a change from gentile to believer; rather it was a baptism of Israel itself." Then he adds in a footnote the following: "That is why it is not possible to deduce John's baptism from proselyte baptism. Although there may be a connection in the exterior rite, the two are qualitatively different."[21]

There are others who show no such hesitancy. Marcus Dods, in his article "Baptism," makes a clear-cut observation: "In the same act, then, John excommunicated the whole people, putting them in the position of gentiles who required to be reborn in baptism, and gave them entrance to the coming kingdom."[22]

J. C. Lambert, in his article, "John the Baptist," makes the same observation: "When a Gentile 'sought shelter under the wings of the Shekinah,' it was understood that he was utterly renouncing his past. And John insisted on a like renunciation in the case of candidates for his baptism."[23] What these men are saying is simply that a candidate for the kingdom, regardless of his covenant in circumcision, must make a new covenant in baptism as a gentile does—and mean it.

Commentators in the *Interpreter's Bible* also join in these opinions:

All Israel must humbly submit to be baptized; as if they were heathen, turning out of darkness to the faith for the first time, and so beginning a new life—a demand to which multitudes agreed, though the Pharisees, disputing the premises as untrue of them, had haughtily refused.[24]

Pre-Christ Baptism by the Nephites

It is interesting to discover that this kind of baptism, which was practiced among the Jews in Palestine, has its corollary among the Nephites. There are four aspects to it, three of which may be rationalized one way or the other and dismissed. The fourth one, however, demands acceptance.

1. Before the Lord appeared to the lost sheep of Israel, there was a man named Alma whose mission was similar to that of John the Baptist. His message was:

The Spirit hath said this much unto me, saying: Cry unto this people, saying, Repent ye, repent ye and prepare the way of the Lord, and walk in his paths, which are straight: For behold, the kingdom of heaven is at hand, and the Son of God cometh upon the face of the earth.[25]

2. Alma introduced baptism for the first time on this hemisphere. His counsel was: "Behold, here are the waters of Mormon. . . . And now, as ye are desirous to come into the fold of God. . . what have you against being baptized in the name of the Lord. . .?"[26] The fold of God and not the fold of Israel is clearly indicated.

3. This baptism was by immersion and at its inception was quite similar to proselyte baptism in that the candidate immersed himself. In the case of Alma and Helam, self-immersion took place only at the introduction of the rite. "And after Alma had said these words, both Alma and Helam were buried in the water; and they arose and came forth out of the water rejoicing."[27]

4. This baptism was the sign of a convenant between the individual and God. Alma spelled out the terms of the covenant in such detail that there was no escaping the responsibility of the candidates. That this detailing

was not done by John may be due to the brevity of the New Testament account. Alma said that those who desired, "to come into the fold of God, and to be called his people," must be willing to "bear one another's burdens. . . mourn with those that mourn. . . comfort those that stand in need of comfort. . . stand as witnesses of God at all times, and in all things, and in all places that ye may be in, even until death." Then they could be baptized "in the name of the Lord, as a witness before him that ye have entered into a covenant with him that ye will serve him and keep his commandments."[28]

The puzzling yet amazing aspect of the similarities between proselyte baptism and Book of Mormon baptism, whose principal actors were separated from each other in time and geographic location, is the source of information. We have partially traced the origin of proselyte baptism and are well acquainted with the moving influence behind John's mission. The question is: What is it that brought about such synchronization when Alma was thousands of miles removed from the "fold of God" in Palestine and with no means of communication? There are three possible answers: (1) The whole story was the creation of Joseph Smith in answer to the division of opinion on the subject in his community, such as the critics of the Book of Mormon assert; (2) Alma was a historical figure called of God to deliver his message, such as John was called to do in Palestine; (3) The idea of baptism as a covenant was in existence among the Jews before the captivity and was brought to Ancient America by Lehi and his family and continued to be taught by tradition until Alma revived the practice and wrote it down.

As popular as the first of these three possibilities may be, we have to reject it on the grounds that we know of no religious sect—when the Book of Mormon was written and in the community where Joseph Smith lived—which held to the idea that baptism was a covenant. On the contrary, there appears to have been some resistance among Christian theologians when Edersheim advanced the fact that baptism existed before the days of John the Baptist. Marcus Dods writes: "The question whether the baptism of proselytes was in vogue as early as the time of the Baptist has been laid to rest by Edersheim and Schurer." Those who continue to hold to the theory that Joseph wrote the book in response to nineteenth century debates on the subject of baptism either are prejudiced, never read the book with a prayerful humility, or are completely ignorant of the fact that baptism existed as a religious rite among the Jews before the advent of the Baptist. Thus disposing of this common notion, we are left with the two other possibilities. Either or both of them may be correct, depending on the views of the individual.

This new evidence of a linkage between baptism and the Abrahamic covenant simply adds to the expanding support of the internal message of the Book of Mormon. This, in return, will assist us in finding a meaning for the Lord's Supper.

Christ on Baptism

Our search so far is fruitless unless we find confirmation in the message of our Lord for the change in the sign of the covenant. Of the four evangelists who gave us the history of the Lord, John is the only one who supplied a theological meaning for baptism.[29] The others simply made reference to it. Matthew may be an exception, but his short statement gives implicit confirmation supporting the Christ-Nicodemus dialogue.[30] Our main interest for the present centers around the visit of Nicodemus. To fully understand what is going on between the two, we must know who Nicodemus was, why he risked coming to Jesus by night, and what he wanted.

All students seem to agree that Nicodemus was a member of the Sanhedrin, the governing body of the Jews. Because of this his words carried considerable authority. He did not become an ardent disciple of the Lord but defended him before the Sanhedrin.[31] After the crucifixion he brought spices to embalm the Lord's body.[32] There is also the tradition that after the resurrection Nicodemus was baptized by Peter and John.[33]

There are three possible reasons why Nicodemus came to Jesus under the cover of darkness. The nation was divided on the claims of Jesus, and so was the Sanhedrin. In order to get the truth at first hand and not be recognized by the public, he took advantage of the night.

A second reason may have been the preaching of the Baptist. The community was agog as the result of John's proclamation of the kingdom of heaven. The Pharisees doubted the claim, but the people believed in him. The very anticipation of the kingdom of heaven could have forced Nicodemus to take the risk and find out for himself.

There is a third reason which students do not seem to recognize—the internal conflict between the national interests of the Jews as contrasted with the

135

worldwide interests of the Roman Empire. This created tension among the people, and as a ruler Nicodemus was not ignorant of it. As a Sanhedrinist, he was a scholar as well as a knowledgeable ruler. The history of the Jews from the Maccabean period to his day was a living nightmare. Hardly did the Syrian Empire weaken until the Romans appeared on the governing scene. Finding the nation in such a state of agitation and subjugation, Nicodemus may have gone for advice. After all Jesus, like the Baptist, was preaching the kingdom of heaven. A man like this should know a way out of this seemingly unending struggle.

Peculiar as it may seem, Nicodemus did not say why he came to Jesus at night. All he said at the beginning was the very important admission: "We know that thou art a teacher come from God; for no man can do these miracles which thou doest, except God be with him."[34] In this brief statement lies the recognition of the divine claims of Jesus. Jewish commentators on Deuteronomy 18:18-20 say: "If a prophet begins to prophesy [i.e., who is still unaccredited] gives a sign and miracle, he is to be listened to, otherwise he is not to be heeded."[35] The miracles of Jesus, then, gave him authority, but did Nicodemus recognize Jesus as simply a prophet, such as arose in the history of Israel, or did he recognize him as the Son of God?

Up to this point of recognition there is near agreement among commentators, but then the divergence of opinion multiplies. There are three points on which students conjecture because the answers Jesus gives to Nicodemus' "How?" are not clear. The "how" of the new birth (verse 4), the how of water and

136

spirit (verse 9), and the identity of Jesus created the perplexity. This was bewildering to Nicodemus and may have been the reason why he held back on baptism until after the resurrection.

The New Birth

Though Nicodemus did not give his reason for coming to Jesus, the matter is resolved by the answer Jesus gave to his recognition: "Verily, verily, I say unto thee, Except a man be born again, he cannot see the kingdom of God."[36] The Sanhedrinist was after the kingdom of God—that much was clear—but how could the kingdom be achieved? Nicodemus, who apparently was an old man by this time, thought of physical birth and asked, "How can a man be born when he is old? Can he enter the second time into his mother's womb and be born?"[37]

Edersheim argues that the words "anew" and "again" can be understood as "from above," and this was the cause of Nicodemus' bewilderment. In the marginal reference of the King James translation one finds a note indicating that the word also means "from above." The same appears to be so in the New Revised Standard Version—born from above or from God.

Granting that this is the case, it is not difficult to understand Nicodemus' bewilderment. The idea of new birth came from the Jews but had nothing to do with anything from above. "It is, indeed, true that a Gentile on becoming a proselyte. . . was likened to a child just born." But this was only a simile, according to Edersheim. It did not involve repentance coupled with moral and spiritual regeneration. It meant that "all the old relations had ceased—a man's father, brother, mother, sister were no longer his nearest of kin: he was a new and another man."[38] By virtue of his baptism he became a child of Israel.

Unfortunately Jewish theology was codified and compartmentalized. It was finished and could not be added to. It dealt with one phase of life—the flesh. Jesus and Nicodemus started from one point—the kingdom—but they differed on the concept. To Nicodemus the kingdom—Israel—already existed. He had no conception of anything from above. Did not Moses say, "And ye shall be unto me a kingdom of priests, and an holy nation"?[39] How could it be otherwise? Nicodemus was not trying to be facetious when he asked, "Can he enter the second time into his mother's womb and be born?" That was the only meaning he derived from the words of Jesus. It never occurred to him that Jesus required new birth of him like that of the proselyte. He was to be born into the kingdom through his inward reconditioning. The new birth of Jesus was renovation of the inward life of Israel. Nicodemus had to be born from above to become a child of God, fit for the kingdom. Otherwise, he would remain simply the child of Abraham.

Birth of Water and Spirit

If the question of the new birth was puzzling to Nicodemus, the birth of water and of the Spirit was more so. Here again the two were looking at the way of entrance to the kingdom from different perspectives. Water to Nicodemus was a sign of covenant the proselyte to Judaisim made so he could become a true member of Israel. He was already a member by virtue of his birth. Furthermore, as a high priest he was not defiled so he did not need cleansing for the remission of his sins. Could Jesus have meant that he, Nicodemus, a member of the Sanhedrin, was—in the sight of God—cast out and needed to enter the kingdom through baptism such as a proselyte? The very thought seemed preposterous, yet that was exactly what Jesus meant.

As a teacher Nicodemus should have been acquainted with the prophets, since it was his responsibility to teach what they said. While Israel was still in captivity Ezekiel wrote:

> Then will I sprinkle clean water upon you, and ye shall be clean; from all your filthiness, and from all your idols, will I cleanse you. A new heart also will I give you, and a new spirit will I put within you; and I will take away the stony heart out of your flesh.... And I will put my Spirit within you, and cause you to walk in my statutes, and ye shall keep my judgments and do them. And ye shall dwell in the land that I gave to your fathers; and ye shall be my people, and I will be your God.[40]

If Nicodemus was thinking of the covenants that God once made with Israel, he should have known that the Israelites did not keep their part of the agreement. For that reason Jeremiah[41] prophesied of a time to come when a new covenant would be made, and the Lord would put his law in their "inward parts" and write it in their hearts. That the people of Israel needed a new baptism, new heart, and new spirit may not have entered the mind of Nicodemus, but this is what Jesus meant. Yet with all that Jesus inferred in his remarks Nicodemus did not show any signs of irritation, such as his colleagues displayed after their denunciation by the Baptist.

Nicodemus was driven to Jesus by a force which was not his own. This was the Spirit of God, but Nicodemus was not able to recognize it as such. What he had heard and seen of Jesus was enough to fill him with uneasiness. Somehow his former beliefs were challenged, but he was not quite ready to accept the new. He experienced a measure of spiritual birth, but it was not enough to undo old prejudices and firmly established beliefs. When Jesus answered his query as to how the Spirit operates, Nicodemus had already sensed that Spirit. His soul heard the sound of it, though he was completely ignorant of the source of its origin and of where it was leading him. He could not have stood up for Jesus before the Sanhedrin, and brought spices to embalm his body, without the Spirit of God touching his soul, shaking his former beliefs, and causing him to come to Jesus by night. His question in the ninth verse was a sincere one. A Pharisee understood the law and was a teacher of it. He had no concept of the Spirit. He needed more clarification to outweigh the traditions and rabbinical teachings with which he was reared.

When Jesus answered the question, "How can these things be?" he appeared to be a little irritated with Nicodemus. The very answer he gave was taunting: "Art thou a master of Israel, and knowest not these things?" A teacher of Nicodemus' standing should have known that a divine pledge cannot be carried out without an effusion of the Spirit of God. He had a famous example in the history of the nation of a noted king, David, who trusted in the flesh and fell. Through the Spirit of God the prophet Nathan revealed the hideous crime. From the depth of his soul David asked for mercy and forgiveness, but above all he petitioned the Lord, "Create in me a clean heart, O God; and renew a right spirit within me."[42] If the kingdom of God was to come to Israel and to Nicodemus, there first had to be a complete and sincere confession of guilt. Then a covenant had to be made in the waters of baptism (such as the proselytes made) before there could be an outpouring of the Spirit of God on the nation as well as on the individual.

Nicodemus appears to have had nothing to say after this explanation. Was his silence an evidence of acquiescence or did he still have unspoken reservations? We know that he did not rush to the waters of baptism after the discourse, and the Lord perceived that he was as confused as ever.

Who Is Jesus?

It seems that Nicodemus had reservations on the Messianic mission of the Lord and needed a more logical reason for what Jesus told him. This comes out in the continuing discourse. Jesus was speaking of what he knew, and Nicodemus did not accept his "witness." For clarity the language was couched in earthly terms, but if Nicodemus was trying to reason out "heavenly things" he was in for a disappointment. That stage of understanding has not yet been obtained. It is difficult to understand the divine even though the message is conveyed in human terms. In his Lord's Supper discourse Jesus left Peter, Thomas, and Judas puzzled. As he told Peter, "You can't

141

understand what I am saying to you now, but soon you will understand."

Though Jesus spoke in the language of the day about baptism as a covenant and the Spirit as a motivating guide, Nicodemus was not able to accept this on faith. Jesus spoke in anticipation of what was yet to happen to him on the cross. Nicodemus had no conception of such a thing. In order to satisfy Nicodemus' inquisitiveness, the Lord told him: "No man hath ascended up to heaven, but he who came down from heaven, the Son of man who is in heaven."[43] In these few words he spoke of his divine nature. He was not an ordinary man or a prophet; he was the Messiah, coming from heaven and being yet in heaven. This may have deepened the mystery to Nicodemus, but there was no escape from it. And as "Moses lifted up the serpent in the wilderness" so Jesus was to be lifted up on the cross for the healing of sick humanity.

Did this brief explanation help Nicodemus? Apparently not. He was still unconvinced, although Jesus closed by saying that "whosoever believeth" in him should not perish but "have eternal life." After he saw the demonstration of the love of God on the cross and Jesus' victory over the grave, Nicodemus was baptized. This is where baptism and the Lord's Supper meet—at the foot of the cross and the victory over it, where the body becomes the bread and the blood the wine.

The symbol of the brazen serpent has its corollary in the symbol of manna.[44] In both cases the Lord was speaking in anticipation of the offering of his body for the sake of humanity. Both were intended for the healing and nutriment of the soul. In the last case, the Lord was more direct: "Except ye eat the flesh of the Son of man, and drink his blood, ye have no life in you."[45]

Matthew's Account

Matthew's account of baptism is very illuminating.[46] Whereas the conversation between Nicodemus and Jesus took place before the suffering of the Lord, this instruction to the eleven apostles took place after his death and victory over the grave. If the simile between the brazen serpent and the cross contributed to Nicodemus' bewilderment, the cause was now removed. In John, Jesus spoke in anticipation of establishing his divinity by his suffering.

The most important feature in this lesson is the Lord's statement: "All power is given unto me in heaven and in earth." This could not have been said and accepted before the crucifixion. Many emphasize the commission, "Go ye therefore, and teach all nations, baptizing them . . ."[47] but forget the "all power." Man throughout his history has looked for power, and no civilization has acquired more power than we have. But the power we have acquired is material—at the expense of spiritual power—and now we are afraid it may result in the destruction of our world. Jesus spoke of a completely different power—the power to overcome self. We are our own greatest enemies. The one who can help us to overcome "self" is not the psychiatrist; it is Christ. Once we are convinced of the power of the Nazarene, baptism becomes meaningful. Through baptism we make a covenant with Deity. This was the meaning of baptism to the people of that day, but simply being dipped in the water was not enough. The eleven were instructed to teach those baptized "to observe all things whatsoever I have commanded you; and, lo, I am with you always, unto the end of the world."[48]

First, they were to teach the people that Jesus has "all power." Next, they were to baptize them. Third, they were to teach them to observe *all* that he had taught them. Once these three steps were considered in order and joined together, a covenant took place. The word "covenant" is not mentioned, but this was its implication to the Jews of that time.

That Jesus, like the Baptist, was following a Jewish custom when he insisted on baptism as a covenant cannot be disputed. The difference lies in the fact that, whereas the proselyte to Judaism becomes an Israelite, the proselyte who accepts the risen Lord and his teachings becomes a child of God. He is born from above and is working in the kingdom of God. This is accomplished not only by his baptism but by his observing "all things whatsoever I have commanded you."

It is interesting to sum up the differences and similarities between these three baptisms.

Proselyte baptism had these features: (1) It was by immersion. (2) It was a covenant to both males and females desiring to become Israelites (at times it dispensed with circumcision). (3) The covenanting individual became a bona fide Israelite. (4) Relationship to family, clan, and former associates ceased, and a new name was given. This was considered being born anew.

John's baptism was different. (1) It focused on Israel

144

itself and not on gentiles. (2) It required immersion. (3) The covenant idea was quite implicit. (4) It insisted on moral regeneration through repentance. (5) It was preparatory, conditioning Israel for the kingdom of God. (6) It was also temporary—a preparation for the greater baptism by the Holy Ghost and fire.

The baptism of Jesus, though similar in some respects to the former two, differed vitally from both. (1) It retained immersion, and the idea of the covenant was implicit. (2) Stress was placed on new birth, but this time the birth was from above—from God. (3) The initiate became the child of God. (4) The birth from above placed one in the kingdom of God. (5) For realization of the kingdom, the individual had the message, teachings, and commandments of Jesus to abide by. (6) There were consequences attached to the new birth: the Holy Spirit was to enlighten in the case of obedience, or to bring judgment (fire) in case of disobedience. (7) Even Israelites had to accept this new birth from above if they were to realize the kingdom. (8) Loyalty to the kingdom came above loyalty to all that was held dear by the individual. Otherwise, the kingdom would be fractured.

Jesus apparently did not accept previous baptisms—even though performed in his name—that were not precise, serious, and demanding. This is the inference one derives from the wording of the great commission. The message of the kingdom now is to "all nations," and if the unity of the kingdom is to be protected, "all things whatsoever I have commanded you" have to be respected and obeyed.

A seeming reversal of this rule appears in Mark where the great commission reads: "He that believeth

145

and is baptized shall be saved."[49] The statement is not contradictory when considered within the context of the gospel of Mark. Baptism as a covenant was well understood by the Jews of Mark's time, and the evangelist himself looked at the message of Jesus as the message of the kingdom of God.[50] Consequently, when he wrote of baptism as a saving ordinance he obviously had in mind the current Jewish belief that baptism was a covenant aiming toward the establishment of the kingdom of God. Furthermore, Mark agreed with the other three evangelists that Jesus was considered king of the Jews.[51]

Baptism and the Apostolic Church

Baptism in the apostolic church retained the same meaning as was taught by Christ in the gospels, though the different writers seemingly emphasized differing aspects. Luke, for instance, in the book of Acts, emphasized remission of sins. But as his references are read within the context of his story, the remission of sins appears to be contingent on acceptance of the Messiahship of Jesus and the covenant one makes toward building the kingdom. Thus, when he reported Peter preaching baptism as a saving ordinance, he did so after referring to the prophet David's statement: "God had sworn with an oath to him, that of the fruit of his loins, according to the flesh, he would raise up Christ to sit on his throne."[52] The three thousand who were baptized that day did so because of their conviction that Jesus, by virtue of his resurrection, was the sovereign king sitting on David's throne. The Samaritans were baptized by Philip after hearing him preach "Christ" and the

146

"kingdom of God."[53] The same inference may be drawn from the baptism of the eunuch. It could hardly be otherwise since it followed the baptism of the Samaritans and carried with it the subject matter which led the former to make the covenant. Neither was Paul's baptism lacking in kingdom involvement when he was told to "arise, and be baptized, and wash away thy sins."[54] After that he devoted his life to the preaching of the kingdom of God.[55] Thus here, as in the gospels, once a covenant was made through baptism, sins were remitted on the ground of repentance and building the kingdom of God.

However, when the order is reversed and the emphasis is placed on remission of sins only—to the exclusion of the covenant and the kingdom—harm is done to the message of Jesus. For centuries this has been the case, and the results are seen best in our modern Christian world. Our social, economic, and political problems are taken over by secular agencies of our own creation. The church assumes a supporting, not an initiating role. This is so because, until lately, when the discovery of baptism as a covenant was made, baptism had an intangible value—completely spiritual as opposed to corporeal. Many of the Christians of today cannot see the value of principles once held sacred. The sacraments such as baptism and the Lord's Supper are not so important today when stress is placed on the material. But when the New Testament writers used the word "baptism" they had in mind the goal—the kingdom of God. Sins were remitted because these people had the interest of the kingdom at heart. They covenanted to bring it about.

That which was taken implicitly in Luke was explicitly emphasized by Paul in his letter to the Colossian saints:

> In whom also ye are circumcised with the circumcision made without hands, in putting off the body of the sins of the flesh by the circumcision of Christ; buried with him in baptism, wherein also ye are risen with him through the faith of the operation of God, who hath raised him from the dead.[56]

What Paul was saying was simply that baptism to the Christian was what circumcision used to be to the Jew. As circumcision was a covenant to the Jew, baptism was a covenant to the Christian.

When Paul contrasted ancient circumcision with the circumcision of Christ he certainly did not have in mind the rite mentioned in Luke 2:21. The circumcision of Christ was identified as burial "with him in baptism." Aimless, sinful individuals are buried, and in their stead persons with a vision of the reign of God are raised. This circumcision is of the heart, whereas the old circumcision was of the foreflesh. "He is a Jew, which is one inwardly; and circumcision is that of the heart, in the spirit, and not in the letter."[57]

Paul put the requirements of the circumcision of Christ in various ways. "The sign of circumcision" to Abraham was a "seal of righteousness"[58] or "the keeping of the commandments of God"[59] or "faith which worketh by love,"[60] or a "new creature."[61] Here is his best summation of the subject:

> Therefore we are buried with him by baptism into death; that like as Christ was raised from the dead by the glory of the Father, even so we also should walk in newness of life... knowing this, that our old man is crucified with him, that the body of sin might be destroyed, that henceforth we should not serve sin.[62]

In baptism the old self is buried to rise up and walk in new life which becomes an instrument of righteousness. This is the kingdom.

Paul, in these quotations, made the total benefits of baptism conditional. If we expect to be the children of Abraham we must have the seal of righteousness as he did. Those who feel that they are called of God and are baptized must keep the commandments. If they believe that they are followers of Christ, they should show their faith by love. And if they desire peace and mercy and to be enrolled in the "Israel of God," they must become new creatures. Though the word covenant is not mentioned in these verses, circumcision is. The implication is covenant making.

Briefly, in this chapter, we have seen the establishment of the Abrahamic covenant, its transformation in time from circumcision to baptism, and the legalization of both. We also have seen how John the Baptist and Jesus adopted the baptismal covenant and made it a requirement for entrance into the kingdom of heaven. All of this took place before the Lord's suffering and caused some to doubt the divinity of Jesus. The apostolic church took the same theme after the resurrection. At that time the recognition of Jesus as the Son of God came in. The brazen serpent in the wilderness was a symbol of his suffering, and the manna which the children of Israel ate was another symbol of his nutritive power. Similarly, those of us who approach the table of the sacred Eucharist by virtue of our covenant in baptism receive the same spiritual nutriment. In the following pages we shall discover why this became so.

1. Mosiah 9:39-41; Alma 5:27, Book of Mormon.
2. *Ordinances and Sacraments of the Church*, Herald House, 1962, pp. 22, 60.
3. Genesis 17:1-14.
4. Genesis 17:13.
5. Genesis 22.
6. Jeremiah 7:23, 24.
7. W.O.E. Oesterley, *Dictionary of Christ and the Gospels*, Vol. I, pp. 330-331.
8. Edersheim, *The Life and Times of Jesus the Messiah*, Longman, Green & Co., London, Vol. II, 1898, pp. 745-746.
9. *Ibid.*
10. *Ibid.*
11. *Ibid.*
12. George Foot Moore, *Judaism in the First Centuries of the Christian Era*, Vol. 1, Cambridge; Harvard University Press, 6th impression, 1950, pp. 331-335. In addition to this refer to the translation from German of Emil Schuerer's work *A History of the Jewish People in the Times of Jesus Christ*, Charles Scribner, New York, Division II, Vol. II, Chapter 31, p. 318 ff.
13. Oesterley, *Dictionary of Christ and the Gospels, op. cit.*, pp. 330-331.
14. Matthew 3:1-12; Luke 3:2-19.
15. Matthew 3:5-6.
16. *Josephus*, Book XVIII, Chapter 1.
17. John 1:40-48.
18. Edersheim, Vol. I, pp. 273-274.
19. Matthew 3:9.
20. Edersheim, Vol. I, pp. 271-272.
21. G. C. Berkouwer, *The Sacraments*, Eerdmans Press, Grand Rapids, Michigan, 1969, p. 97.
22. Marcus Dods, *Dictionary of Christ and the Gospels*, Vol. I, Scribners, p. 170.
23. J. C. Lambert, *Dictionary of Christ and the Gospels*, Vol. 1, p. 863.
24. *Interpreter's Bible*, "John's Baptism," Vol. 8, p. 506.
25. Alma 5:17, 18, Book of Mormon.
26. Mosiah 9:38-41, Book of Mormon.
27. Mosiah 9:45, Book of Mormon.
28. Mosiah 9:39-41, Book of Mormon.
29. John 3:1-15.
30. Matthew 28:16-20.
31. John 7:50, 51.
32. John 19:39, 40.
33. *Smith Bible Dictionary*, Little, Brauen and Co., 1865, Boston, p. 619.
34. John 3:2.
35. *Interpreter's Bible*, Vol. 8, p. 503.
36. John 3:3.
37. John 3:4.
38. Edersheim, Vol. I, pp. 384-385. The new birth was commonly

accepted in ancient Judaism, and the idea came with the Nephites to this land. Ether does not mention it. (See Mosiah 11:186-188; 11:190; Alma 3:27, 86; 5:24; 13:49; 17:5, 21, 23.)

39. Exodus 19:6.
40. Ezekiel 36:25-28.
41. Jeremiah 31:31-33.
42. Psalm 51:10.
43. John 3:13.
44. John 6:22-65.
45. John 6:53.
46. Matthew 28:17-19.
47. Matthew 28:18.
48. Matthew 28:19.
49. Mark 16:15.
50. Mark 4:24; 9:1, K.J.; 10:13, 24; 12:39.
51. Mark 15:29.
52. Acts 2:30.
53. Acts 8:6-12.
54. Acts 22:16.
55. Acts 14:22; 19:8; 28:23.
56. Colossians 2:11, 12.
57. Romans 2:29.
58. Romans 4:11.
59. I Corinthians 7:19.
60. Galatians 5:6.
61. Galatians 6:15.
62. Romans 6:4, 6.

CHAPTER SIX

REDEMPTION AND THE COVENANT

Our forefathers had the tendency to take a complicated subject such as the Lord's Supper and connect it with the Jewish Passover. For this reason they taught that a covenant was made with Israel in Egypt, hence the Lord made a covenant with his disciples as he ate the last meal with them in the upper room. Actually, the subject is so tangled that it needs clarification before an assertion can be made. It may be shocking to some to discover that there was no covenant made in Egypt. All that took place there was deliverance and redemption. The covenant was made at Sinai. The same is true of Christianity. The covenant, as far as man is concerned, is made in baptism and not in the eating of the Lord's Supper. In the last meal in the upper room Jesus was establishing, in advance, the redemption which he was to offer for the human family through the shedding of his blood. He still was not the redeemer. The trouble with Nicodemus was not that he did not understand the meaning of the baptismal covenant. He did, and as a rabbi he must have taught it. His difficulty was, *with whom* was he making the covenant—with a prophet or with the Messiah? The divinity of Jesus had not yet been fully established.

To become valid a covenant needs attestation by two signatories. In our own everyday terminology we say that a covenant needs *countersigning* to become lawfully binding. Man's sign of accepting the covenant of Jesus is signified by his baptism. Should we not expect a counter-signature from the heavenly Father giving authority to the man, Jesus of Nazareth? To the Jews he was an ordinary person, "the carpenter's son,"[1] or, "the son of Joseph whose father and mother we know."[2] This was not only the question of nearly two thousand years ago; it is the question in the mind of many a person today: *Who is Jesus?* Is he a prophet, an outstanding teacher, or the Messiah? The heavenly Father does not expect us to covenant with one whose divinity is not proven. This is best illustrated by the dealings between God and man in the deliverance from Egyptian bondage.

The Redemption of Israel

It was commonly understood by our ancestors, and before the advent of biblical criticism, that the Lord's Supper and the covenant involved in it were an answer to the Jewish symbolism expressed in the Israelitish Passover and the Paschal Lamb. Now we know differently. What we read of happening in Egypt was the deliverance of a few thousand slaves by the mighty arm of God.[3]

The story begins with Moses and the burning bush, the commission to go to Pharaoh, Moses' complaint, the call of Aaron, and the ten punitive measures inflicted upon the Egyptians. The word "covenant"

153

in connection with those to be delivered was not mentioned. It was used, however, to remind them that God had previously covenanted with Abraham their father and was now fulfilling his promise.[4] Instead, one finds the terms "deliver"[5] and "redeem from" heavy bondage of Pharaoh.[6] The Israelites had been enslaved so long they were not able to understand Moses and had completely forgotten their God. Their spiritual strength was totally sapped from them, and the majority appear to have accepted their fate. By the strength of the mighty hand of God they were delivered from their taskmasters for a purpose yet to be revealed.

The worst, however, was still ahead of them. They hardly had time to rejoice over their escape when they discovered that the Egyptians were still in pursuit. This time they had no room to maneuver. In front of them was the Red Sea, behind them was the Egyptian army, and on either side was the lifeless desert. If the ten plagues were not enough to convince them of the divine power behind their deliverance, this escape would.

And Moses said unto the people, Fear ye not, stand still, and see the salvation of the Lord, which he will show to you today.... And the Lord said unto Moses, Wherefore criest thou unto me? speak unto the children of Israel, that they go forward.[7]

The waters of the sea were divided, and the people walked through to the northeast side on dry land. The Egyptians followed, but the waters went back together and the mighty army was drowned. The fifteenth chapter is the victory song of Moses. Throughout these chapters the story of redemption is stressed.

154

The Sinai Covenant

Three months after their deliverance from the Egyptians, the people of Israel were camped at the foot of Mt. Sinai. It was here that the Lord made a covenant with them.[8] It was here also that the law was given. The setting was ideal for the occasion. Next to the mount there was a low hill, and the space between resembled an amphitheater. After the people were settled the Lord spoke to Moses out of the mountain:

Thus shalt thou say to the house of Jacob, and tell the children of Israel; Ye have seen what I did unto the Egyptians, and how I bare you on eagles' wings, and brought you unto myself. Now therefore, if ye will obey my voice indeed, and keep my covenant, then ye shall be a peculiar treasure unto me above all people; for all the earth is mine; and ye shall be unto me a kingdom of priests, and a holy nation. These are the words which thou shalt speak unto the children of Israel. And Moses came and called for the elders of the people, and laid before their faces all these words which the Lord commanded him. And all the people answered together, and said, All that the Lord hath spoken we will do.[9]

The whole affair was a solemn religious transaction. Nothing was done in the dark, and there was none of what we call "fine print" hiding ambiguous intentions. The Lord began with the obvious: "You have seen what I did to the Egyptians, and how I bare you on eagles' wings." The question is: Why should the Egyptians suffer and the Israelites be redeemed? The first half of the question is not directly answered, but the second half is. The Lord did this to make Israel his property—the people of God. As such they were to be made a kingdom of priests and a holy nation to the peoples of the earth, including the Egyptians, because all the earth is the Lord's. They were to minister to others so they could be brought under the lordship of God.

This was not a new thought to the Israelites though they may have forgotten it. God had previously disclosed it to Abraham: "And in thy seed shall all the nations of the earth be blessed; because thou hast obeyed my voice."[10] Abraham was faithful to the covenant he made, even when his only son was requested for a sacrifice.

The Lord had in mind first the nations of the earth, and second Israel—the first to receive ministry and the second to minister. The Israelites accepted the task and answered: "All that the Lord hath spoken we will do." As a go-between, Moses "returned the words of the people unto the Lord." With their acceptance of the mission a covenant could be made.

The mountain then had to be made ready for the reception of the Lord. A thick cloud covered the top of it, and there was lightning accompanied by the sound of trumpets. Then came the smoke and quaking of the mountain. The phenomenon was terrifying to the people. Undoubtedly this was intended to reinforce the fact that the God of Israel had power even over the forces of nature. Following this the ten commandments and other instructions were given to guide the conduct of the people. All the details were spelled out. Moses recited the message, and the people answered a second time: "All the words which the Lord hath said will we do."

With this accomplished, he ordered the erection of an altar and twelve pillars below the hill. Then he requested animal sacrifices for burnt offerings. He took the blood of the beasts and divided it into

156

two portions. One he poured on the altar, and started reading again from "the book of the covenant." Then, for the third time, the Israelites answered: "All that the Lord hath said will we do, and be obedient." Following this commitment, Moses took the other portion of blood and sprinkled it on the people, saying, "Behold the blood of the covenant, which the Lord hath made with you concerning all these words."[11]

It is common knowledge now that they did not live up to the agreement they made. And, as previously stated, Jeremiah condemned them as covenant breakers and assured them that the Lord their God would make a new covenant with them.

Thus confronted with the facts, we come to the conclusion that the covenant was made at Sinai, not in Egypt. All that happened in Egypt was deliverance.

Christ—The Deliverer

Similarly and logically we have to look for redemption in the New Testament narrative before we can make a covenant. As Moses opened his covenant address to the people by saying, "You have seen what God did to the Egyptians" before the covenant was made, we have to see what God did to our enemy before we can enter into covenant relationship with him. The redemption we speak of here was fully realized in the completion of the mission of Jesus of Nazareth. Although the people—and worse than that, his immediate followers—did not understand his mission, somehow after the crucifixion and resurrection the message began to dawn upon them. It is the apostolic church which gave us the full impact of Christ's redemption for the world.

But before we look into the apostolic account we should first consider the gospel narrative. Prominence in this respect is given to the gospel according to Luke which contains in detail prophecies in this connection not mentioned in the other three. When dispute arose as to what to name the child born to Zacharias and Elizabeth, the dumb father opened his mouth and called him John. Then he prophesied, saying,

Blessed be the Lord God of Israel; for he hath visited and redeemed his people, and hath raised up an horn of salvation for us, in the house of his servant David.... And thou, child, shalt be called the prophet of the Highest, for thou shalt go before the face of the Lord to prepare his ways.[12]

Jesus came from the line of David while John descended from Levi. Simeon, a devout man, empowered by the Holy Ghost, at seeing the baby Jesus in the temple cried out, "Lord. . . mine eyes have seen thy salvation, which thou hast prepared before the face of all people."[13] And Anna, a devout woman who attended the blessing of Jesus, spoke of him as bringing "redemption in Jerusalem" (or, as the marginal reference states, redemption to "Israel").[14] Matthew gives the name of the child before his birth and adds: "He shall save his people from their sins."[15] The Baptist, according to the gospel of John, points out Jesus to his followers and says: "Behold the Lamb of God, who taketh away the sin of the world."[16]

Jesus on His Mission

More important than the prophetic insights others had on the mission of Jesus is the matter of how Jesus looked upon his own mission. Since the subject we are dealing with is redemption, we should not fasten our attention on the term. Only once is the word attributed to him (in connection with his second coming).[17] Instead we should check his sayings to discover the meaning in context.

Immediately after his baptism by John, Jesus had the Spirit descend on him in the form of a dove, and he heard a Voice saying: "Thou art my beloved Son, in whom I am well pleased."[18] Matthew's account is slightly different; according to it the voice was heard by observers at the baptism.[19] Whether the announcement was heard by Jesus only or by both him and the audience, he was called "my beloved Son." And as the Son of God visiting the earth, he was not on a sight-seeing tour; he came to save.

Following his baptism and confirmation Jesus withdrew to the wilderness where he fasted for forty days. Here he was tempted three times by the devil.[20] There is a difference in the accounts by Matthew and Luke in the order of the temptations, but in two of them the devil said: "If thou be the Son of God . . ." Jesus' knowledge that he was the Son of God was still restricted to him. The public, including his own disciples, were not aware of it. Only when he and his disciples reached the region of Caesarea Philippi did his identity become known to his immediate followers.[21] First, he put them to the test by asking what people thought of him. Their answer was simple: he was a prophet like John the Baptist, Elias, or one of the other prophets. Then, he addressed the question to them: "But whom say ye that I am?" Peter answered, "Thou art the Christ, the Son of the living God." This disclosure was important. In the first two cases—

the baptismal scene and the temptation—Jesus was called the Son of God. In this case he was identified as the Son of the living God. That was a time of many gods. Roman emperors were proclaimed gods. The Greeks and other pagan nations had their peculiar gods. Only Israel had a living God. This made Jesus more than a prophet and more than the popularly expected Jewish Messiah. Even his mission was greater than what was expected by the Jews of that day.

With his own disciples aware of his identity, Jesus was ready to disclose his mission. He was to go to Jerusalem, where his claims would be rejected by the elders, the chief priests, and the scribes. This would lead to his suffering, crucifixion, and his resurrection from the grave after three days interment.[22] These statements regarding his mission at the beginning of his ministry were followed by the institution of the Lord's Supper at the conclusion of that ministry.[23]

All of the preceding citations are disputed by students, and I may be held guilty of oversimplifying them. John's account, however, because of the support it received from the Book of Mormon, is one that believers in this "latter-day Scripture" may rely on. It makes the subject much clearer. "As Moses lifted up the serpent in the wilderness, even so must the Son of man be lifted up; that whosoever believeth on him should not perish, but have eternal life."[24] As Israel was anciently enslaved by Egyptian princes, Jesus looked at the world as being enslaved by the devil: "Now is the judgment of this world; now shall the prince of this world be cast out. And I, if I be lifted up from the earth, will draw all men unto me."[25] Worse than that, not just the world—which did not know God—but the Israelites—the children of Abraham who made a covenant with God—were enslaved by their "father the devil," and only "the Son" could make them "free indeed."[26] All of these quotations infer the saving power which belongs to Jesus.

It is distressing that neither the Jews nor Christ's own disciples understood his mission. Even Peter, the one who recognized him as the Son of the living God, rebuked him when he spoke of his ultimate saving mission.[27] Peter could not conceive of the sacrifice Jesus was making for the sake of humanity. He had the old Jewish concept of "King Messiah" over Israel. Mark puts it differently: "They understood not that saying, and were afraid to ask him."[28] Luke recorded the same conversation of the Lord with his disciples: "And they understood none of these things; and this saying was hid from them; neither remembered they the things which were spoken."[29] It is little wonder that some of them went fishing after the Crucifixion.

All of these quotations refer to a divine plan leading to the salvation of mankind through the suffering, death, and resurrection of the Lord. They are best summed up with the short but decisive statement: "For the Son of man is come to save that which was lost."[30] The same statement was repeated by Luke,[31] although the setting in which it was made differed from the one mentioned by Matthew. The demonstration of Christ's saving mission offended the Pharisees at times. On one occasion they saw him eating with publicans and sinners. They taunted his disciples with "Why eateth your master with publicans and sinners?"[32]

On another occasion, Luke reported the mission of the Lord as preaching good news, healing the broken-hearted, releasing the captives, restoring sight to the blind, and preaching the acceptable year of the Lord.[33] Again, the implication was clear. He was quoting Isaiah[34] in support of his saving claim. The case was mentioned again by Matthew[35] and Mark[36] but with some significant differences which disturb the critics. This, however, should not detract from the subject. These men did not know shorthand and could not record exact utterances. The fundamental issue is that they all agreed on the quotation from Isaiah. They also agreed that the audience was offended. The offense may have been because Jesus claimed such a sweeping, saving power. Both Matthew and Luke reported the parable of the lost sheep.[37] Jesus came here to save.

I have omitted purposely the statements of Jesus which were uttered in this connection at the Lord's Supper because they were under careful scrutiny. The fact of his predictive death is not questioned. It is the chronology of events leading to his self-sacrifice that is debated. The Synoptics and John agree that he ate a meal with the twelve, and that he told them of his impending death, though they had hardly any understanding of what he was saying.[38] The wording which John used was different from that used by the Synoptics. But there is no mistaking the fact that Jesus spoke of his betrayal,[39] the lack of understanding of his disciples of the coming tragedy,[40] and of his death.

Redemption and the Apostolic Church

Dazed, bewildered, and scattered after the crucifixion, the disciples of Jesus were in no position to assess the impact of Calvary. What may have stunned them was the popular belief that the Messiah would not die but would live forever.[41] Peter and a few with him went back to their occupation—fishing. Their confusion, however, did not last long. Soon the news began to filter out from different sources that Christ had arisen from the grave and had appeared to some of his followers. As the evidence of the resurrection was multiplied, the disciples rallied around the twelve and met in Jerusalem. It was here that the identity of Jesus became associated with the Redeemer, though the word was not used. Thus the resurrection became the pivotal point in Christianity.

The Redeemer's Credentials

With unmatched courage Peter, who had denied his Lord three times in the hall of judgment, stood before the assembled crowd on the day of Pentecost and said: "God hath raised up" Jesus who was "crucified and slain." He insisted that although Christ had been placed in a grave, his body saw no "corruption." Peter further emphasized, "We all are witnesses" of this resurrection. It is natural that an unprecedented announcement such as this, accompanied by the effusion of the Holy Spirit, would produce fear and self-examination in those listening. With the resurrection of Jesus from the grave, God was literally in their midst through the Spirit. Were they worthy and what should they do? Peter's answer was plain and comforting: "Repent, and be baptized every one of you in the name of Jesus Christ for the remission of sins, and ye shall receive the gift of the Holy Ghost."[42]

163

Peter could have had the words of Jesus to Nicodemus in mind when he offered this solution. "For God sent not his Son into the world to condemn the world; but that the world through him might be saved."[43] By virtue of his resurrection, Jesus Christ became the savior of mankind, but if this salvation is to be achieved it must be on the grounds of sincere and genuine repentance accompanied by the baptismal covenant.

On three different occasions following Pentecost, Peter maintained his position on the saving ministry of Jesus. In the case of the curious people on Solomon's porch when the impotent man was healed, he attributed the recovery to faith in the name of Jesus Christ, glorified by God as he was raised from the dead.[44] When Peter stood before the council to give an answer as to how the lame man was healed, he said, "By the name of Jesus Christ of Nazareth, whom ye crucified, whom God raised from the dead, even by him doth this man stand here before you whole." Then he concluded with the far-sweeping statement, "There is none other name under heaven given among men, whereby we must be saved."[45] The same declaration was made to Cornelius and his Italian company. Word of the risen Lord had already reached them, and what Peter did was to confirm the good news. He was an eyewitness because he ate and drank with the risen Jesus. And Jesus further commanded them "to preach unto the people, and to testify that it is he which was ordained of God to be the Judge of quick and dead" and "that through his name whosoever believeth in him shall receive remission of sins."[46]

In two of the preceding references (Acts 2:38; 10:43) resurrection from the dead is a voucher for the remission of sins to the penitent and covenanted believer. This is in agreement with the last commission of the Lord recorded by Luke.[47] This consistency in style and wording in Acts carries over to cover the ministry of Paul. In the first sermon preached after his ordination, Paul announced that Christ arose from the dead after his cruel death and through him "is preached unto you the forgiveness of sins."[48] In his epistle to the Roman Saints, Paul called himself an apostle of Jesus Christ who was "declared the Son of God. . .through the resurrection from the dead."[49] Yet he wrote about the newness of life of the baptized individual, speaking of sins remitted by the burial of "the old man."[50] In his epistles to the Ephesians and Colossians he used the word "redemption" as being identical with forgiveness of sins.[51] The problem of wording does not alter the substance of the message. Consequently, the conclusion presented in the book of Acts is that through the fact of the resurrection of Christ from the grave, redemption is offered to the human family.

It may have been noted from the preceding that there is no mention of the cross and blood of Christ in these early writings. This is so because those who were associated with Jesus in his ministry looked at the resurrection as embodying the cross and blood of Christ. Without the cross and the blood there could have been no resurrection. And without the resurrection, the blood and the cross would have been meaningless and devoid of any saving significance.

Later, as opposition to the message of the apostles

began to develop among the Jews, every phase of the death of the Lord which had as its basis prophetic statements of the past was brought to bear on the argument. Peter for example, wrote to the church saying: "Who his own self bare our sins in his own body on the tree, that we, being dead to sins, should live unto righteousness; by whose stripes ye were healed."[52] The hanging on the tree reminds the reader of Deuteronomy 21:22-23. The implication is clear. Christ became a curse for us. Paul used the same reference.[53] The healing "by his stripes" takes us back to Isaiah's suffering one.[54]

While all writers of the New Testament agreed on the redemptive mission of Jesus, none of them emphasized it as strongly and in such sophisticated terms as Paul in his letter to the Romans. He appeared as the outstanding defender of the universality of the saving mission of Christ. The Roman congregation was composed of both Jews and gentiles. There may have been theological tensions between them. Scholars do not seem to agree on a single motive behind the letter, but this tension may have served as the motive. The feature on which there appears to be no disagreement, however, is the highly reasoned presentation on the mission of Jesus.

Introducing the Atonement

Paul approached the subject by stressing the universality of the sin of mankind: "For all have sinned and come short of the glory of God."[55] This sin entered into the race through Adam's disobedience.[56] Paul repeated this in his letter to the Corinthians: "For as in Adam all die, even so in Christ shall all be

166

made alive."[57] For this reason none are justified before God—not even those who have the law and boast of works.[58] Man can only be justified "only by his grace through the redemption that is in Christ Jesus; whom God has set forth to be a propitiation through faith in his blood, to declare his righteousness for the remission of sins that are past" that "he might be just, and the justifier of him which believeth in Jesus."[59] The thought is carried over into the fifth chapter where the word "atonement" is introduced.[60] The reason that sins are remitted through the death of Jesus is that people might be brought to God: "We were reconciled to God by the death of his Son; much more, being reconciled, we shall be saved by his life."[61] Such an individual becomes "a new creature,"[62] a "new man"[63] reconciled to God, and by virtue of this, to him is committed the ministry of reconciliation.[64]

It is fitting that the Fathers who assembled the books of the New Testament concluded the collection with the Revelation of John. It is only in this book that Christ is identified with the Paschal Lamb before whom the representatives of humanity and the angelic hosts sang, "Worthy is the Lamb. . .for thou wast slain, and hast redeemed us to God by thy blood out of every kindred, and tongue, and people, and nation."[65] The anthem has been repeated by successive people at different times, showing the appreciation of obedient humanity for the saving power and sacrifice of Christ.[66]

My purpose here is simply to give enough evidence—without exhausting the subject—to show that from the apostolic period until the middle of the last century the church held fast to the belief that Christ was the redeemer of mankind. The Pauline compact formula that "Christ died for our sins according to the scriptures; and that he was buried, and that he rose again the third day according to the scriptures" became the dictum of the Christians.[67]

The Turning Point

The preceding is true only when one considers the general belief of the Christian. The story of the theological battle which arose around the fact of redemption is completely different. The Christians of the first two hundred years were not interested in whether they would be saved by the cross, the blood, or the death of Jesus. The fact of the resurrection was the single historical declaration on which they based their belief. The cross and the blood were ignominies perpetrated against Jesus, but in the resurrection he obtained the victory. To them it was enough to know that Jesus was the Son of God, and that he taught a message of salvation involving this world and the world to come. They regarded themselves as brothers from the moment of conversion; they had a common fund for the help of the unfortunate among them; and—when persecuted—they died for their belief instead of compromising with either Rome or the Jews. Worldly goods were means to an end, and not ends in themselves. If the letters to the seven churches (Revelation 2-3) can be used as a criterion for their belief, one can safely say that works, faith, and perseverance characterized their lives to a very large extent.

Somewhere around the second and third centuries

theologies began to develop which ultimately brought the whole subject of redemption into disarray. There are two words in the New Testament around which the battle rages—"ransom" and "propitiation." First, let us consider ransom.

The word was used by Matthew and Mark.[68] Later on it was used by the apostle Paul in his letter to Timothy.[69] Paul complicated the problem by using the word "atonement" to describe the death of Christ.[70] In doing so he was drawing on his Jewish background. Ransom and atonement were closely connected. The Old Testament atonement carried with it the payment of ransom.[71] The amount of money was specified as half a shekel (about five dollars) to be paid once a year by each of the children of Israel, twenty years and older, as "ransom for his soul." When writing to Timothy Paul referred to Jesus as mediator between God and man, "who gave himself a ransom for all." Thus the connection was unmistakable, and a proverbial hornet's nest was created. The tragedy of it is that we have no way of knowing whether Paul used the word in a literal or figurative sense. The conclusion was that the devil kidnapped man and God had to give Jesus Christ for a price so that man could be retrieved. Horrible as the thought is to us now, this was the interpretation given to the atonement for nearly eleven hundred years. Some think that this theology was advanced by Irenaeus or Origen after him, but the attribution is not that well defined. One thing we know: this theology was accepted as the teaching of the church until Anselm originated the satisfaction theory. This, however, did not end the debate; theories began to multiply and have continued to do so down to our day.[72]

The word "propitiation" appears only three times in the New Testament and not at all in the Old Testament. It was used by Paul and the writer of the first epistle of John.[73] The meaning is similar to ransom. Among pagans the word meant the payment of money or the offering of a sacrificial victim in order to placate an individual or a deity. Its use in the New Testament has always been a source of controversy. For eleven hundred years it has been synonymous with ransom, suggesting to theologians of the period that God allowed his Son to become a sacrificial victim as a payment for the release of man from devilish captivity. With the coming of the period of scholasticism, this theological monstrosity was overwhelmingly rejected, but no satisfying formula has met with unchallenged reception. Its use by Paul has created more controversies than anything else he wrote.

Even though many students attribute the first epistle of John to the author of the fourth gospel, there are those who challenge the conclusion. Among their many reasons is the presence of this word in the epistle. If the fourth gospel and the first epistle of John were written by the same man, then why was the word not used in the fourth gospel? Debate on the issue is academic and should concern us only because of the light which it sheds on the harmony between the gospel of John and the Book of Mormon.

Tradition and Doubt

We are now reaching the crucial point in this study.

Are the story and act of redemption historically real, or did the story develop in between the actual death of Jesus and the time when it was written? During this period of tradition the story of Jesus grew and ultimately became gospel. At this point debate, scholarly assertion, and refutation rage but with no decisive conclusion. It would seem that the scale is tipping in favor of the negative, however. To the masses of the young the Jesus story is an entertaining subject. Witness to this is the musical, *Jesus Christ, Superstar.* To knowledgeable people, there is emerging interest in an obscure pre-Christ literature which may, in the opinion of those bringing it to light, discredit the fact of atonement and the resurrection.[74] As will be subsequently seen, however, its emergence is a blessing (in my judgment). When this literature is compared with the Book of Mormon account, it gives support to the New Testament idea of an atonement and resurrection.

There are students, on the other hand, who do not submit to such absurd ideas as this literature presents. They seriously believe that Jesus was the Messiah by virtue of his sacrificial death and resurrection. Their position, however, is weakened when they are confronted with such words as "propitiation" and "ransom." They attribute their presence in the Christian message either to a mistake or faulty interpretation. For this reason expiation is substituted for propitiation in the Revised Standard and the New English Bibles.[75] And where ransom appears in the King James, Revised Standard Version, and the New English Bible, it is part of the phrase, "as a ransom." (There is one exception: the New English Bible renders

171

I Timothy 2:6 in such a manner that the word ransom does not appear at all: "Who sacrificed himself to win freedom for all mankind.") Noble and acceptable as these changes are, at best they inject a note of uncertainty in the Christian witness.

The Book of Mormon Story

The Book of Mormon account is steeped with prophetic utterances made in anticipation of the coming of the Messiah and his atoning mission. It is this frequent teaching about the atonement which arouses suspicion in the minds of modern students. Here one finds a full-blown Christology before the advent of Christ which seems to have no parallel among Palestinian Jews of the same period. Are these prophecies in the Book of Mormon faked—or true as the book claims? If true, do they shed any light on these two words which have rocked Christian theology for the last seventeen hundred years?

These predictions of the coming of Christ and his atoning mission are true and shed light on the bothersome question of "ransom" and "propitiation." The criticism of a pre-Christ Christology is based on the assumption that we know all there is to know about Jewish life and especially the background which preceded the coming of Jesus. There has been no evidence from Jewish annals foretelling such an atonement as the Book of Mormon speaks of. The Dead Sea Scrolls, however, blasted this assumption, and there is emerging new archaeological evidence that rabbinic Judaism suppressed any movement which was contrary to the legal and rational interpretation of the Mosaic law. Michael Stone, in *Scientific America* for January

1973 concerning new finds of ancient synagogues covering a period from 200 B.C. to A.D. 100, wrote:

If one were dependent on only the writing transmitted within the Jewish tradition, our knowledge of Judaism around the times of Christ would be sparse indeed. Information about those groups that rabbinic Judaism opposed has been systematically ignored or suppressed in rabbinic writings.

Then he summed up the article in these words:

Both Jewish and Christian scholars had tended to evaluate evidence of varieties in Jewish religious expression in terms of their orthodoxies. Jewish scholarship had underplayed the mystical, speculative and other non-rational aspects of Judaism. The result was rather a limited picture of the rabbinic Judaism that has emerged triumphant after the temple in Jerusalem had been destroyed by the Romans in A.D. 70.[76]

Even Schonfield, who bases his conclusion on insufficient evidence behind a Passover plot, admits:

It is not easy to throw light on these pre-Christian ideas of the Jewish eclectic groups because much of their teaching was not made public and the literature to which we have access is somewhat mysterious in its expressions.[77]

Evidence supporting the authenticity of a pre-Christ Christology in the Book of Mormon is proved by the absence of ransom and propitiation in any connection with the atonement. This is startling, especially when one considers that these words were in popular usage when the Book of Mormon was translated. Latter Day Saints often sing a Communion hymn inspired by the prayer the Lord taught his disciples to repeat on the emblems.[78] It is ascribed to W. W. Phelps who joined the church nearly two years after the Book of Mormon was first printed. He used sublime phrases and words from that prayer such as "bless and sanctify," "witness," and "have his Spirit." But he also made a serious mistake by using the word "ransom." The reason for this is that he was inspired by the new prayer language, but by tradition and usage he was still attached to old beliefs. Here is the third stanza of the hymn:

When Jesus, the Anointed, descended from above
And gave himself a *ransom* to win our souls with love,
With no apparent beauty that men should him desire,
He was the promised Savior, to purify with fire.

Phelps would not have used ransom in his hymn had the word not been popular in his day. Such a familiar term could easily have been used by Joseph Smith in connection with the atonement had he been the power behind the translation of the Book of Mormon. (A reverse argument is that if the word was so common and was accidentally used by W. W. Phelps, what would have prevented the accidental use of it by Joseph Smith?) It is reasonably evident that the absence of the two offending words was by divine intention. Thus, once again the Book of Mormon affirms its divine claim as "the fullness of the gospel," and the redemptive mission of Jesus Christ finds another support, completely independent of the theological teachings of the day.

Satisfying as this may sound, the Book of Mormon introduces the word "appease" which, if not correctly understood, may cancel what clarification is contributed to ransom and propitiation.[79] According to Webster's Dictionary, appease comes from an Old French word, which meant "to bring a state of peace"—hence any legitimate effort bringing peace. Most commonly, however, it is understood as pacifying by dubious means. This we have to reject. In this case it is used in connection with justice. God is both merciful and just. From the very beginning the Book of Mormon account states that "men are instructed sufficiently, that they know good from evil." There is "opposition; even the forbidden fruit in opposition to the tree of life. . . . Wherefore, the Lord God gave unto man, that he should act for himself."[80] When the first parents of the human family disobeyed they with their posterity were "cut off from the presence of the Lord."[81] Therefore, it was expedient that mankind should be reclaimed from this spiritual death. How this reclamation should take place is the question: would it be by an act of mercy or an act of justice? If by an act of mercy, then what would happen to the justice of God? He would lose his character. If by justice, then the wrong should be redressed and justice appeased (put at peace). Through the atonement this peace was established. "Therefore God himself atoneth for the sins of the world[82] . . . and bringeth back men into the presence of God"[83] on grounds of repentance.

This same thought was uppermost in Paul's mind when he wrote: "Therefore being justified by faith, we have peace with God through our Lord Jesus Christ."[84] This peace was synonymous with the word "reconcile" which Paul used in the same chapter and also in his letter to the Corinthian saints.[85] He made himself much clearer, however, in his letter to the Ephesians:

But now, in Christ Jesus, ye who sometimes were far off are made nigh by the blood of Christ. For he is our peace, who hath made both one, and hath broken down the middle wall of partition between us . . . and came and preached peace to you which were afar off, and to them that were nigh.[86]

Thus as God redeemed Israel through Moses to

175

eventually make a covenant with them, so God again accomplished through the vicarious death of Jesus Christ the redemption of the human family on the grounds of repentance and baptism, the latter being a sign of the covenant. It is hoped that in case of any hesitancy on the part of the participant in the Lord's Supper because of some confusion over the credentials of the redeemer, the source of confusion is now removed.

THE FALL AND ATONEMENT CLARIFIED

The Book of Mormon further deals with a singularly unique topic which has a definite bearing on the subject. It presents a paradox however, on the matter of the creation of evil and righteous propensities in man.[87] The statement stands alone; it has no parallel in either the Old or New Testaments. For this reason, perhaps, it has inspired doubt.[88] It is both philosophical and theological, and in this sense no one can attribute it to the nearly unlettered boy of Palmyra. In order to understand its unique significance, we have to consider first the origin of good and evil inclinations.

When man was created as a person, there simultaneously was created in him "opposition; even the forbidden fruit in opposition to the tree of life" (vv. 97, 98). Thus the tendency for good and evil exists in man; the devil merely entices—he does not create evil. The purpose of this creation was that man "should act for himself." He could choose either the bitter or the sweet, the good or bad. He was to act for himself and *not to be acted upon* (v. 118). Thus, as a responsible individual, man was a free agent capable of making moral choices. He did not have to listen to the devil, but, since he did, he brought about his own fall.

The implications of this philosophy are far reaching. Consider the statement that man "is not to be acted upon." If this is true, then man could not be kidnapped by Satan, as our forefathers believed, unless he allowed himself to be. Because of this there was no need for "ransom," and the Book of Mormon account presents none.

Also consider what this does to the dualism which Christianity inherited from Christian Gnosticism. It shatters the very concept. We can't have monotheism and dualism. Such ideas do not mix. This does not mean that there is no devil. There is, but he is not coequal or cocreator with God. He is a fallen angel. He tried to "entice" the Lord but did not succeed. As angels do materialize to the eyes of man,[89] Satan also could materialize into an angel of light.[90] Joseph Smith struggled physically with such a power, but its force was not to be compared with the power of the two personages who subsequently appeared to him. In a day of theological extremes, it seems to me that we are forced to take a stand. We can't keep being tossed from the demonology of the middle ages to the negation of the devil, as has happened during this intellectual period, and then back to demonology, exorcism, and even devil worship, as is being reported among a small section of the young. If devilish possession does take place, the individual himself is responsible. Because of carelessness in his religious duty he gradually allows himself to be possessed.

The most interesting observation is still to be considered. Man is not influenced by only one force. He is to be "enticed by the one or the other" (II Nephi 1:100). Adam did evil because he listened to the fallen angel. Who is to entice man to do good? All he knows now is his evil inclinations. This is a one-sided agency, which in reality is no agency at all. But the account continues: "And the Messiah will come in the fullness of time, that he may redeem the children of men from the fall" (II Nephi 1:116) or from this one-sidedness. This is the second half of the statement and should not be missed. Thus the atonement had a double purpose— to atone for the Adamic sin and to set Messiah as an enticing example to be followed.

Paul had a similar thought when he explained the meaning of the death of Christ for humanity. "For the love of Christ constraineth us."[91] The word "constrain" implies force, while "entice" implies tempting or alluring, but both of these words are used in the sense of attracting.

The next question that naturally comes to mind is this: How did the concept of the creation of good and evil enter into the Book of Mormon text? The Holy Scriptures do not present such a clear-cut statement. The answer is very plain in view of ancient Jewish writings. Consider this:

178

Jewish authorities. . . teach that man is created with two inclinations—that to evil (the Yetser ha-ra), and that to good; the first working in him from the beginning, the latter coming gradually in course of time. . . . In fact as the Talmud expressly teaches, the evil desire or impulse was created by God himself; while it is also asserted that, on seeing the consequences, God actually repented having done so.[92]

There appeared no thought in the mind of the writer that an atonement was proposed to overcome the Yetser ha-ra. Instead "study and works" were suggested by which Israel could conquer evil inclinations, such as was done once before "at Mount Sinai."[93]

It is clear that the idea of the creation of good and evil propensities in man came with the members of Lehi's family as they left the land of Jerusalem. Lehi obtained the information from his reading.[94] Did he read Jewish commentaries, or did he read the Scriptures which were brought with them? While we think that he secured his knowledge from the last, the first is not to be ignored. To this also may have been added a measure of inspiration. In his debate with Sherem, Jacob refers to the Scriptures for the first evidence of an atonement, and then to the manifestation of the Spirit.[95] King Benjamin, while lecturing on the coming of the Messiah and his atonement, opened his remarks by declaring that "the things which I shall tell you, are made known unto me, by an angel from God."[96]

Evidence of the Scriptures

When we examine the Old Testament for supporting evidence of the divine creation of good and evil in man we encounter a scarcity, but there is one statement from Isaiah which more than compensates. (I am indebted to Elder F. Henry Edwards for calling it to my attention.) "I form the light, and create darkness; I make peace and create evil: I the Lord do all these things" (Isaiah 45:7). Detached from the Talmudic background, it might not convey the full meaning, and this could lead to difficulties. We would easily attribute arbitrariness to this action of God, but the God of Israel was neither capricious nor willful: "He [spoke] righteousness," and declared "things that are right" (verse 19). This may have led the exegete in the *Interpreter's Bible* to write: "The evil which God creates is not moral but physical, like disaster. . ." which is partly correct, but he ignored the fact that in creating man God placed the inclination for both good and evil in him. When the aggregate of national action tends toward evil, disaster follows. Such was the case in the Babylonian captivity. The God of Israel was preparing the way for the redemption of his people, and Cyrus was the man chosen for deliverance.

This verse also leads to pleasant surprises. Chapter 45 of Isaiah is one of eight dealing with the return of the exiles to their homeland (40-48). Because of the predictive nature of their message they are assigned by the majority of students to what is known as Second or Deutero-Isaiah. They are supposed to have been written about the year 538 B.C. when Cyrus issued the edict for their return. The original Isaiah lived and prophesied about 200 years before this time. His active prophetic period covered about fifty years—from 740 to 690 B.C. When Cyrus issued the declaration the real Isaiah was already dead, hence it was assigned to an unknown individual called Second Isaiah. The prophet, the critics reason, is a man who speaks to his people in his own time. He does not predict long-range events.

The majority of statements taken from Isaiah and included in the Book of Mormon are from this supposed Second Isaiah. Since Lehi and his company left Palestine 600 years B.C., this unspoken and unwritten portion of Isaiah could not have come with them. Hence the Book of Mormon to the critic is false.

This criticism, however, should not be a disturbing factor. We have already seen how contradictions in the gospel account were corrected by the "fullness," and critical views were overturned. The same holds true here. The argument for the division of Isaiah is an apparently sound argument to self-sufficient man, but here we are dealing with a divine plan of fullness. How can we account for the harmony between the Book of Mormon pronouncement on the divine creation of evil and the terse statement of Isaiah? I can see some apparent objection such as Jewish traditions which could have been behind both, but we have no record of such a tradition. The formation of the Talmud began in Babylon after Isaiah was dead. This makes it obvious to me that Isaiah was a unit before the migration from Palestine to the Americas such as it was discovered to be a complete unit 200 years before Christ among the Dead Sea Scrolls and just as it is a unit today. Regarding the predictive element on which students base part of their judgment for the division of the prophecy, however, we must remember that we are dealing with predictions when we apply the omniscience of God as found in the Book of Mormon to the solution of perplexing theological problems. Such foreknowledge as we have already found in the course of our investigation is indeed past our intellectual dreams and imaginations; It is divine; it is miraculous.

The Blindness of the Jews

What is interesting here is that there were no insights among the Jews for a universal Messianic atonement such as existed among the Nephites in ancient America. They did not deny atonement; they merely denied its universality and its connection with the Messiah. Edersheim says:

> There is, indeed, in Rabbinic writings frequent references to the sufferings, and even the death of the Messiah, and these are brought into connection with our sins—as how it could be otherwise in view of Isaiah 53, and other passages.... But there is only the most indistinct reference to the removal of sin by the Messiah in the sense of vicarious sufferings.... The final result is far from that seriousness which attaches to the Fall in the New Testament.... [97]

What is astonishing in the light of this is the Jewish performance of atoning services for the gentiles. These were done in the temple during the Feast of Tabernacles. Seventy bullocks were sacrificed for the nations. Once the temple was destroyed and the altar gone, however, the Jews lamented the cessation of the atoning act.[98]

Thus the Israelites became confused about priorities. Their souls were completely ignored. They were preoccupied with national sovereignty and their relation to other nations. When they thought of Messiah (and they were steeped in this concept) they thought of "King Messiah." Their problems were best detailed by Josephus. From their Babylonian return until the destruction of the second temple their activities centered around national difficulties. There were wars, and some of the leaders and high priests became

182

corrupt. There was oppression and persecution of dissidents (this is revealed in the Dea Sea Scrolls. The Teacher of Righteousness was persecuted and sent into exile. The harsh disciplinary measures of this community served as an atonement for the "earth and ensuring the requital of the wicked"[99] (the wicked here refers to the Jewish oppressors).

The loss of sight of a worldwide mission and of the purpose of the Messiah is gleaned from the question the eleven disciples asked of Christ after the resurrection: "Lord, wilt thou at this time restore again the kingdom to Israel?"[100] Because of their Rabbinic indoctrination, these disciples were looking for a "King Messiah" who would restore the dignity and power of Israel as a nation among nations. After Pentecost they saw their mission differently. Thus, because of the blindness of their hearts, there were no prophets in Israel who saw the atoning mission of Messiah as the people of America saw it.

Schonfield's Mistake

In support of his thesis, Hugh J. Schonfield seizes on what he calls the "eclectic" writings (pseudepigrapha) of Jewish commentators to strengthen his case.[101] In the chapter titled "The Suffering Just One and the Son of Man," he quotes from the testaments of the Twelve Patriarchs, the Book of Jubilee, and other literature of the period, attributing the atonement and resurrection of Jesus to a Syrian myth adopted by the northern kingdom of Israel which, in turn, assigned its origin to Joseph the son of Jacob. From the northern kingdom the myth went to the southern kingdom and finally was adopted by the Christian church. True, the people of Israel came in contact

183

with the Syrians. From them the Jews could have learned of the Syrian god, Adonis-Tammuz. It was said that he was wounded, died, and arose from the dead. He also became the god of the cult of fertility. In verification of the transfer of this myth from the Syrians to Israel, then to the southern kingdom and to the church, Schonfield refers to an apparent legend of Joseph to whom was attributed the origin of the Day of Atonement. (If Schonfield's statement is true, and we have no evidence to the contrary, then it is not surprising to find such an abundance of references to the atonement in the literature Joseph's descendants left us on the Americas.) He then concludes by saying:

> In Jewish teachings Joseph was the perfect righteous man, whose brethren persecuted him and attempted to get rid of him. But in the providence of God he who was humiliated was afterwards exalted and became the savior of the sons of Jacob from whom he had been separated.[102]

The question is, "Savior from what—famine or sin?" The only answer the record gives is famine.[103]

It is fortunate that Schonfield bases his thesis on suspicion. The facts are completely different. Compare the foregoing statement with what Nephi said regarding his father's genealogy.

> He was a descendant of Joseph; yea, even that Joseph who was the son of Jacob, who was sold into Egypt, and who was preserved by the hand of the Lord, that he might preserve his father Jacob and all his household from perishing with famine.[104]

The difference here is in wording, not in substance. According to the best knowledge we have, the children of Israel were "saved" from famine. Nephi gave the same account but used the word "preserve" instead of save. Considering the distance in time and space as well as the similarities between the two accounts, we are forced to conclude that a legend of Joseph existed. But how can we account for the analogous presence of this legend in the American Scripture? Just as the idea of the creation of good and evil came with the Nephites from their former home, this legend must have come with them also. The discovery is exciting, because there is no rationale by which we can connect it with western New York theology of the early nineteenth century.

Nephi did not have to go that far in identifying his father's genealogy. He could have said, "Joseph, the son of Jacob," and everyone would have understood. Or he could have said "Joseph who was sold into Egypt by his brethren," and that would have been sufficient. But by indicating that he was the preserver of his father Jacob and his household, he apparently was referring to the legend. Its existence in the southern kingdom must have predated 600 B.C. when Lehi and his family left the land of Palestine. The literature Schonfield quotes had its beginning around 200 B.C. (and some think later than that). Its authors are supposed to be Jews of the Pharisaic sect noted for their conservatism. Thus the antiquity of the legend plus the fundamental nature of the Pharisees throws considerable doubt on the suspicion that it had its sacred origin in a Syrian myth which was adopted by the northern kingdom.

The Shepherd and Stone of Israel

In addition to the preceding theory, Schonfield refers to Joseph's patriarchal blessing in which Jacob says "from thence is the shepherd, the stone of Israel."[105]

Again, he uses this prophecy to show how extensively Messianic predictions were spread in the days of Jesus. Acquainted with this literature, Jesus came to the conclusion that he was the expected Messiah-Shepherd, while in reality the shepherd and stone were connected with Adonis-Tammuz-Adad prior to their adoption into the religious system of Israel, thus causing the delusion of Jesus.

The blessing, however, is complicated and confusing. It appears to be made up of two prophetic combinations, and if it is to be properly understood it should be divided into its component parts. First we should deal with the stone symbol; second, with the shepherd symbol; and third, with the blessing as it now stands.

The Stone

The stone symbol may have come to Israel from the Syrians or any of their other neighbors. This, however, is no proof that its use by Israel, and more especially by Jesus, was the result of a deluded mind. Both the Psalmist and Isaiah used the symbol prophetically, and Jesus applied it to himself.[106] Where the symbol came from is not important. In a small and closely connected geographic area where Syria, Palestine, and Egypt are located, it is easy for idioms peculiar to one country to be transferred to the other. The important thing is the sacred aura the prophets of Israel gave to the symbol. It is not clear how the Psalmist used the symbol, but there is no doubt about its use by Isaiah. He applied it to Jerusalem and its rulers (28:14). Apparently they made a covenant with neighboring nations with the result of accepting their deities but this was no evidence of security. It was a covenant with death and hell, resulting only

186

in judgment. Then he gave his prophetic forecast: "Therefore thus saith the Lord God, Behold, I lay in Zion for a foundation a stone, a tried stone, a precious corner stone; a sure foundation: he that believeth shall not make haste." This forecast was fulfilled in the mission of Jesus. The New Testament writers used the symbol as proof of the divinity of Jesus.[107] It is this proof which Schonfield scorns. A New Testament student, he is well acquainted with the results of the gospel criticism which reduced Jesus to the human level. What he has done in his book is to add the finishing touches by suggesting that the account was fraudulent, but the use of the symbol was genuine.

The Shepherd

The shepherd symbol goes back to Isaiah.[108] The Lord refers to no scripture as he applies the symbol to himself, but all Christian students see its fulfillment in Christ Jesus. Indeed, it was a bold declaration when he said, "I am the good shepherd.... And other sheep I have, which are not of this fold; them also I must bring, and they shall hear my voice; and there shall be one fold, and one shepherd."[109] These statements are unique in gospel literature. They have no parallel in the synoptic account. For this reason there has been a prolonged debate as to what was meant by these sayings, especially the "other sheep."

The appearance of the symbol in the Book of Mormon excites curiosity but also helps in the solution of the problem.[110] "Other sheep" refers to that branch of Israel which was guided to the Western Hemisphere. When the Gospel of John was under attack by the critics and when its origin was placed in the second half of the second century I had reservations about using this text. Also when references to the Christ-shepherd in the Book of Mormon stood alone, without support given to the internal message of the book, I could see that skepticism would be natural. Now, however, since the discovery that the Gospel of John was written by the son of Zebedee, and we have seen sufficient harmony between this gospel and the Book of Mormon, I do not hesitate to say that the statement as uttered by the Lord is authentic. It found its fulfillment in Christ's visit to the Nephites.

What gives an added boost to this conviction is the literature to which Schonfield refers. Both his quotes of the Joseph legend and the shepherd and stone came from the pseudepigrapha. I doubt that a satisfactory answer for his accusation can be found outside the Book of Mormon. Verification of the Joseph legend came from the descendants of Joseph; the same applies to the shepherd and other sheep.

Another factor worthy of consideration is the nature of the two civilizations in the Book of Mormon. The words under discussion are conspicuously absent from any connection with deity in the Book of Ether. Joseph Smith wrote both under inspiration. Had he been depending on his own ingenuity and Christian background, the words used in the Nephite account would have appeared in the Jaredite story. Thus, in view of all the evidences, the Schonfield thesis appears to be baseless.

Joseph's Patriarchal Blessing

This conclusion may appear unfair, however, unless

we take a look at the whole blessing of Joseph. It must be understood from the vantage point of the time in which it was given; otherwise we will be led into difficulty. What we have analyzed already is the one quotation, "from thence is the shepherd, the stone of Israel." There is more to the blessing which appears to be contradictory to what we have already resolved. Schonfield does not dwell on this seeming contradiction, but other students do.

There are those who consider the statement, "from thence is the shepherd, and stone of Israel," to mean that the Messiah will come from the direct descendants of Joseph. Yet Jacob in this chapter was giving each one of his children a blessing. When he pronounced the blessing on Judah[111] the promise was made that Messiah (Shiloh) would come from his seed. If we are to take these words literally there is naturally grave contradiction. The exegete in the *Interpreter's Bible* appears to have fallen into this temptation. He considered the original blessing of Joseph consisting of one verse, the twenty-second only. The other verses were added by a "succession of writers to stress the pre-eminence of the Joseph tribes. In this its final form it contradicts verse 8, according to which Judah has the leadership of the nation."

If we have learned one thing from our study of baptism it was that in Israel there were two kinds of births: the person born of the blood line of Abraham, and the gentile adopted through baptism as a bona fide Israelite. The adopted individual was referred to as born again and newly born. Customs then were radically different from ours; to judge them by our standards would be wrong. Take for instance the custom of a man dying without male progeny. His brother married the widow, and the male born to the marriage belonged to the dead man rather than to the one who fathered him.[112] John the Baptist was considered by the Lord as Elias, yet Elias had been dead for years.[113] John simply came in the spirit of Elias. Because of Reuben's transgression, his birthright was taken away and given to Joseph.[114] It is in this sense that we understand the words, "from thence is the shepherd, the stone of Israel." Jesus came from the blood line of Judah, and Joseph's blessing did not contest the fact. It simply stated that from Joseph's progeny there would come the propagating evidence that the Jesus of Judah would indeed be the Messiah. This was a rebirth when for all practical purposes the Messiahship of Jesus was dead.

A major purpose of the Book of Mormon is the illumination of obscure and conflicting accounts in the New Testament. Aggregate evidence produced by this study tends to support this claim. It also removes the tendency among some students who attribute the book to a concoction of Smith's eclectic mind. Theological interest during the early part of the nineteenth century, when the book was written, centered on the harmony of the gospel account, not on its contradictions. Neither was there debate, as far as I know, on the date, origin, and wording of the Lord's Supper—and certainly not on baptism as a covenant and the ramifications of the story of redemption.

Thus, in the utter absence of any option out of which Smith could have had a choice for the construction of the account, we have to fall back on the divine origin of the Book of Mormon and reject Schonfield's thesis. Though it appears beyond human comprehension, God ordained that when the Messiahship of Jesus would be protested by both Jew and Gentile, out of Joseph's seed there would come a new and convincing evidence that Jesus is the Christ, the eternal Redeemer. The pre-Christ Christology of the Book of Mormon is the result of the special endowment which was promised them.[115]

Consequently, we conclude that if Schonfield's statement in the Pseudepigrapha is true, and we have no evidence to the contrary, then it is not surprising to find such an abundance of references to the atonement and shepherd in the literature Joseph's descendants left us on the Americas.

Thus, anyone having the right to participate in the Lord's Supper by virtue of the covenant he or she made in the waters of baptism should not be influenced by the slight errors the critics discovered in the New Testament account regarding the redemptive act of Jesus. The distracting features are astonishingly corrected in the record of the Nephites. One should always keep in mind that the Book of Mormon account preceded the critic's discovery and the popularization of the discrepancies. Though human mistakes entered the former text, the illimitable love of God is seen behind both accounts. God loved the world through the redemptive sacrifice of his only begotten Son two thousand years ago and is still loving humanity now by clarifying that which is ambiguous or wrong. As guests at the meal partake of the bread and wine, they are eating and drinking with confidence, knowing that the account of a redeemer in the New Testament is true though mistakes entered into it in the course of time. By correcting the account, the heavenly Father has fulfilled his obligation toward man. Next, we should look for the obligation of man toward the redeemer.

1. Matthew 13:56.
2. John 6:42.
3. Exodus 3:15.
4. Exodus 6:2-8.
5. Exodus 3:8.
6. Exodus 6:6; 13:14.
7. Exodus 14:13, 15.
8. Exodus, chapters 19-24.
9. Exodus 19:3-8.
10. Genesis 22:22.
11. Exodus 24:8.
12. Luke 1:67, 68, 75.
13. Luke 2:29-31.
14. Luke 2:36-38.
15. Matthew 1:21, K.J.
16. John 1:29.
17. Luke 21:27.
18. Mark 1:9.
19. Matthew 3:13 ff, K.J.
20. Matthew 4:1-10; Luke 4:1-12.
21. Matthew 16:14-21; Mark 8:28-31.
22. Matthew 16:21.
23. Matthew 26:26-29; Mark 14:20-22; Luke 22:19, 20.
24. John 3:14, 15.
25. John 12:31, 32.
26. John 8:31-43.
27. Matthew 16:22-24.
28. Mark 9:29.
29. Luke 18:34.
30. Matthew 18:11.
31. Luke 19:10.
32. Matthew 9:12.
33. Luke 4:16-19.
34. Isaiah 61:1, 2.
35. Matthew 13:54-58.

36. Mark 6:1-6.
37. Matthew 18:12-14; Luke 15:1-7.
38. Matthew 26:26-29; Mark 14:22-24; Luke 22:19, 20.
39. John 13:21.
40. John 13:28.
41. John 12:34.
42. Acts 2:38.
43. John 3:17.
44. Acts 3:12-18.
45. Acts 4:12.
46. Acts 10:42, 43.
47. Luke 24:45, 46.
48. Acts 13:38.
49. Romans 1:4.
50. Romans 6:6.
51. Ephesians 1:7, Colossians 1:14.
52. I Peter 2:24.
53. Galatians 3:13.
54. Isaiah 53:5.
55. Romans 3:23.
56. Romans 5:12-15.
57. I Corinthians 15:22.
58. Romans 3:20, 27.
59. Romans 3:24-26.
60. Romans 5:8-11.
61. Romans 5:10.
62. II Corinthians 5:17.
63. Ephesians 2:15.
64. II Corinthians 5:18 ff; Ephesians 2:10-16.
65. Revelation 5:12, 9.
66. Revelation 7:10, 14-17; 12:7-11; 14:1-4; 19:6-9.
67. I Corinthians 15:3, 4.
68. Matthew 20:28; Mark 10:45.
69. I Timothy 2:5-6.
70. Romans 5:11.
71. Exodus 30:10-16.
72. The subject is best summarized by James Orr in his article "Redemption," as it appears in *Dictionary of Christ and the Gospel*, Vol. II.
73. Romans 3:25; I John 2:2; 4:10.
74. Hugh J. Schonfield, *The Passover Plot*, Bantam Books, 1966.
75. For a clearer understanding of this change, one should become acquainted with C. H. Dodd's commentary on *The Epistle of Paul to the Romans* first published by Hodder and Stoughton, London, then printed in Fontana Books.
76. I am indebted for this information to Dr. and Mrs. Jeremy Baptist, who—knowing of my interest in the subject—provided me with this material.

77. Schonfield, *The Passover Plot, op. cit.*, p. 207.
78. *The Hymnal*, p. 260, Herald House, Independence, Missouri, 1956.
79. Alma 19:97.
80. II Nephi 1:67, 97-99.
81. Alma 19:90.
82. Alma 19:97.
83. Alma 19:105.
84. Romans 5:1.
85. II Corinthians 5:18-19.
86. Ephesians 2:13-14, 17.
87. Nephi 1:97-121.
88. Chris B. Hartshorn, *A Commentary on the Book of Mormon*, p. 96.
89. I Nephi 3:50.
90. II Corinthians 11:14, 15.
91. II Corinthians 5:14.
92. Edersheim, Vol. 1, p. 167. See also Isaiah 45:7.
93. *Ibid.*
94. II Nephi 1:101.
95. Jacob 5:16-21.
96. Mosiah 1:93-107.
97. Edersheim, Vol. 1, p. 165.
98. *Ibid.*, p. 168.
99. *The Dead Sea Scriptures*, Anchor Books, Garden City, N.Y., translated by Theodore H. Gaster.
100. Acts 1:6.
101. Schonfield, *The Passover Plot*, Part 2, Chapter 3.
102. *Ibid.*, p. 210.
103. Genesis, chapters 42-47.
104. I Nephi 1:165.
105. Genesis 49:24; Schonfield, *The Passover Plot, op. cit.*, p. 210.
106. Psalm 118:22; Isaiah 28:16; Matthew 21:42; Mark 12:10; Luke 20:17.
107. Ephesians 2:20; I Peter 2:6.
108. Isaiah 40:9-11.
109. Jonah 10:11, 16.
110. III Nephi 7:16-23.
111. Genesis 49:8-12.
112. Deuteronomy 25:5-10.
113. Matthew 11:12-15; 17:9-14.
114. I Chronicles 5:1.
115. The blessing of Joseph as given by his father does not stand alone. Moses gives his blessing to the twelve tribes and Joseph is included (Deuteronomy 33:13-17). Its similarity to the blessing given by Jacob is striking. But it also omits "from thence, is the shepherd

the stone of Israel." Why the omission, while other like features are stressed, is puzzling. Did the author fall into the temptation thinking of two biological births for Joseph? Hardly so. He was well acquainted with the new birth of adoption into Israel. Perhaps the answer lies in the rivalry between the northern and southern kingdoms. It is a known fact among students that the Pentateuch is composed of more than one document. Deuteronomy did not appear on the scene until the reign of Josiah, king of Judah (II Kings 22-23). By that time the northern kingdom had ceased to exist. The book was discovered as the priests were cleansing the temple from foreign deities. There has been extensive debate on its origin. Some think the book is a fraud. Others think because of the similarity of its phraseology with Jeremiah, it appeared around the Jeremiah period. There are others who attribute its origin to the nothern kingdom. Our concern, however, centers not on its debatable origin but on the omission of "from thence is the shepherd, the stone of Israel." Due to discoveries which have already appeared in the course of this study, we are made to wonder if there may have been suppression in this case such as Mr. Stone mentions (see page 173). Jewish writers of the period were acquainted in the Qumran community (some reference to Dead Sea Scrolls) but their literature ignored it. The question becomes more pressing because of a vital change in the *Targum Onkelos*, page 70. The problem is: How much can one rely on rabbinical writings?

195

CHAPTER SEVEN

OBLIGATIONS OF THE COVENANT

Participation in the Lord's Supper is more than a religious ceremony involving only devotion to God and to the memory of Jesus. If anything is being made clear in this study, I hope it is the obligation of the covenanting individual to keep Christ's commandments. The importance of this was emphasized during the Lord's Supper discourse in Jerusalem, reported only by John. The same thing took place when Jesus appeared to the Nephites and taught them the consecration prayer on the emblems. The priest petitions God that the covenanting participants may be "willing to take upon them the name of thy Son, and always remember him and keep his commandments." All of this is involved in the baptismal covenant to do, to observe, to keep. Jesus kept his Father's commandments and expects his followers to do the same.[1] The thing that led him to the cross was his unswerving devotion to the instructions of his Father.

The preceding becomes more significant when we consider the word "sanctify" in the opening petition of the consecration prayer on the emblems. The object of this sanctification is the soul—not the bread and wine—that the one partaking may remember Jesus and keep the commandments which he has given.

On another occasion when the Lord consecrated the twelve in Jerusalem he used the same word: "Sanctify them through thy truth: thy word is truth." Again, sanctification is connected with the word and cannot be considered as an incidental happening. But what is the word? Is there any clear understanding of it? (See Chapter 4.) Before the age of biblical criticism, division of the Christian sects was structured along the line of how the word was understood. That was when the word was considered inerrant; the story is different now, and great latitude is taken in interpretation and application. It appears to me that just as there are model-years for cars, appliances, hair and dress styles, there are also model-years for theological thinking. The stress now is on unity regardless of the word, but there are also faint signs that a reversal of the trend is beginning to take place. Liberal churches are dying while conservative ones are gaining.[2] This is bound to make some difference.

Fortunately for us (and for all Christians who are willing to listen) the words, commandments, and teachings of Jesus are made clearer in his message to the Nephites. Just as perplexing issues connected with the Lord's Supper were solved, identification of his commandments will be solved also. Then, if they are implemented in the lives of those who made the covenant, the horrifying tragedies now facing civilization can be averted. These commandments will be explored under two different headings: those teachings derived from the example of Jesus as he encountered opposition or faced issues, and his direct teachings as reported by Matthew and Luke.

Jesus as a Criminal

In order to understand the indirect teachings of Jesus we must remember that he was regarded in some of the influential circles of his time as a criminal. This was because of his devotion to the commandments of the Father. He observed them to the letter and was eventually crucified for them. Paul injected this thought when he wrote: "For he hath made him to be sin for us, who knew no sin; that we might be made the righteousness of God in him."[3] Paul conceded that Jesus knew no sin, yet he was made sin for us. This does not mean that his agency was taken away from him—he had it until the very end—but in obedience to God's commandments he was treated as a sinner. He made no compromises. Likewise we, if we obey the commandments and imitate the example of Jesus, will become the righteousness of God for others to behold. Modern humanity, faced by the perilous horrors of the day, has no alternative but the teachings and commandments of Jesus to save it.

The Guilt of Jesus

The guilt of Jesus to his accusers stemmed from his teachings and treatment of humanity. To Jesus man was flesh and spirit,[4] or body and soul.[5] In saying this he was following old beliefs, namely, that man was composed of matter and spirit.[6] This combination made him a potential son of God.[7] In the fourth gospel this concept was accepted, with sonship limited

198

to the reception of Jesus: "As many as received him, to them gave he power to become the sons of God." These "were not born of blood, nor of the flesh...but of God."[8] Thus the relationship between God and man is similar to the father-son relationship. Its best spiritual expression is made in communion between the two. For this reason Jesus said: "If a man worships God, he must worship him in spirit and in truth;...for the Father seeketh such to worship him."[9] Hence the invitation comes from the Father seeking man to commune with him. The idea of God as Father was well known to the Jews[10] but not taken seriously. The result was that they failed to recognize his representative on earth (John 8:47).

As a child of God, man was priceless in the eyes of Jesus. He was like a lost sheep from the fold of God and needed to be recovered,[11] or like a lost penny from a woman's purse which must be found.[12] By cutting himself off from communion with his Father, man would become helpless, and the Father without the child would be lonely.[13] While the Jew looked at the law as being above man, Jesus put man above the law. Man was not made for the Sabbath, but the Sabbath was made for man.[14] The Jews objected to a deed of mercy being done on the Sabbath, but Jesus healed the impotent man on that day.[15]

Man as a Spiritual Being

As a spiritual being, man was endowed with discerning faculties. This was his agency, his freedom of choice. He could serve either God or mammon, but not both.[16] The things belonging to Caesar should be given to Caesar, but the things of God should be rendered to God.[17]

Man has a spiritual eye capable of being focused. If it is focused on God, his whole body will be full of light. If it is focused on evil, the whole body will be full of darkness.[18] The man who chooses wealth as his only life's purpose is a fool. He loses his soul:[19] "For what is a man profited, if he shall gain the whole world, and lose his own soul?"[20]

The Heart in Man

When it came to personal righteousness or the lack of it, Jesus turned to the heart as the wellspring of spirituality. To him the heart was more than the physical organ which forced the blood to the extremities of the body. It was the seat of all moral and spiritual discernments. Adultery was more than committing an illicit sexual act. According to him anyone who lusted after a woman had already committed adultery in his heart.[21] To those who would stone a woman because she committed adultery and was caught in the act, he said, "He that is without sin among you, let him first cast a stone at her." When he said this, the accusers disappeared.[22] Contrary to Jewish beliefs, to eat with unwashed hands was not sin. Jesus said that defilement originated in the heart, and its results were "evil thoughts, murders, adulteries, fornications, thefts, false witness, blasphemies."[23] People such as publicans and sinners with whom the Pharisees would not associate were spiritually sick people, and it was his duty as a physician of the soul to be with them.[24] Only the pure in heart would see God.[25]

Man and Evil

It is interesting to note that Jesus never called man a sinner. He ate with sinners and associated with them. The real enemy was the devil. For this reason Jesus came to destroy the very stronghold of evil and keep it cleansed.[26] In the Lord's prayer, he taught his followers to pray: "Deliver us from evil." He came to cast out the prince of this world.[27] He aroused the ire of the Jews most when he accused them of not being free; they were of their father the devil.[28]

Man and Self

The decisive issue between the Jews and Jesus came to a head when he challenged their exclusiveness by his universalism. The Pharisees abhorred not only publicans and sinners but the foreigners such as the Greeks and Romans. Worse than this, they detested their relatives, the Samaritans. Jesus' own disciples were not free from this national prejudice. When an Italian, a centurion, came to Jesus for help in healing a stricken servant, to justify his deed of mercy, Jesus said "to them that followed, Verily, I say unto you, I have not found so great a faith; no, not in Israel."[29]

The same thing is inferred in his conversation with the Syrophoenician woman.[30] There is a slight variation between Matthew's account and that of Mark. Students are not all in agreement as to why Jesus compared her to a dog, but some draw a conclusion from the comparison. The children are those who belong to the covenant, while the dogs represent the gentiles. This is made clearer in Matthew's account.

Also by making this comparison, Jesus may have assuaged the national feelings of his own disciples.

The biggest offense, however, took place in his own town of Nazareth.[31] Here he dared to elevate the foreigners above the Jew. "Many widows were in Israel in the days of Elias...but unto none of them was Elias sent, save unto Sarepta"—to a foreign widow woman. "And many lepers were in Israel, in the time of Eliseus the prophet; and none of them were cleansed, save Naaman the Syrian." Such statements were inflammatory, and the people did not take them lightly. They thrust Jesus out of the city and took him to the cliff to cast him down, but he escaped.

When we look at man as Jesus saw him, we discover a very vital reason for his redemptive sacrifice. Neither Moses, Mohammed, nor Buddha attached such value to man as Jesus did. Women were created for the enjoyment of men as far as some religious leaders were concerned. Only in the sight of Jesus were male and female considered equal—not because of their physical makeup but because of the spiritual qualities placed in them. The more humanity ignores the sacrifice of this man for its betterment, the more it shall drift into slavery, serfdom, and self-destruction. This is man as Jesus saw him, and the covenanting believer is to imitate this example.

Eternal Life

In addition to his revolutionary concept of the worth of man, Jesus advanced the view that life was eternal. The Jews knew only of sheol—the place of the dead—the grave.[32] In Job there appears the suggestion that life might be eternal,[33] but some think of this statement as simply a hope—nothing more. The words "eternal life" do not appear in the Old Testament. In the teachings of Jesus, however, life is considered eternal and there is no doubt about it. If man is a spiritual being, the spirit does not die as the body does.

On one occasion Christ was approached by a man who asked, "Good Master, what good thing shall I do, that I may have eternal life?" The question is recorded by all the Synoptics.[34] In addition to these three recordings, Luke makes another statement on the subject which is independent of the others.[35] All of these statements concern eternal life. They also appear to be abrupt, having no connection with previous conversations. Does this abruptness suggest that the subject was so widely taught by Jesus that the Synoptics recorded only the dramatic incidents? The lawyer who put the question to him was apparently attempting to lay a trap. In the King James account the words "tempt him" are used, and in the Standard Revised Version, "A lawyer stood up to put him to the test." This indicates that the subject was widely used by Jesus in contradiction to what the Jews believed, else why should the lawyer put him to the test? The answer is obvious: to ridicule him and to alienate his huge following.

It should be noted here that eternal life in the preceding references is connected with life in the kingdom of God. Those who value material wealth above eternal life cannot inherit the kingdom. Jesus also connected the kingdom of God with his own person.[36] Those who rejected him rejected the kingdom. For this reason he told the chief priests and the elders, "The kingdom of God shall be taken from you, and given to a nation bringing forth the fruits thereof."[37] The fulfillment of this prediction cannot be denied; the kingdom was given to the gentiles. At the same time it should serve as a warning to those among us who are strong on the rhetoric and hope of Zion but short on working toward its actual accomplishment.

The fourth gospel tells a different story. It is replete with statements concerning eternal life. The term, "kingdom of God" appears only twice in it,[38] and this in connection with the visit of Nicodemus. Instead of "kingdom" the words "life," "light," "the way," and the "truth" are used, and all of them are inseparable from the person of Jesus. In the opening chapter it is stated: "In him was life; and the life was the light of men."[39] Later Jesus is reported as saying, "I am the way, the truth and the life," and he that "seeth the Son, and believeth on him, may have everlasting life."[40] And the Baptist is reported as saying, "He that believeth on the Son hath everlasting life: and he that believeth not the Son shall not see life; but the wrath of God abideth on him."[41] Some argue, with justification, that these utterances do not refer to life past the grave but rather to the bliss and peace which follow the believer in this life, beginning with his conversion. A life tied to Jesus and his cause is a life of joy and bliss, and if this is so here, it becomes continuous life beyond the grave. He made this clear when he said:

He that heareth my word, and believeth on him who sent me, hath everlasting life...for the hour is coming, in the which all who are in their graves shall hear his voice, and shall come forth; they who have done good, in the resurrection of the just.[42]

Except for a slight difference in wording this is in agreement with the Synoptic account. When Peter said, "We have forsaken all, and followed thee; what shall we have therefore?"[43] Jesus answered (in Mark's account), "There is no man that hath left house, or brethren, or sisters, or father, or mother, or wife, or children, or lands, for my sake and the gospel's, but he shall receive an hundredfold now in this time...and in the world to come, eternal life." Luke put it differently: "Who shall not receive manifold more in this present time, and in the world to come life everlasting."

It is in this sense that we understand his statement to the Samaritan woman: "The water that I shall give him shall be in him a well of water springing up into everlasting life."[44] The same is also true of the many references in the sixth chapter:

The bread of God is he which cometh down from heaven, and giveth life unto the world (verse 33).
And this is the Father's will which hath sent me, that of all which he hath given me I should lose nothing, but should raise it up again at the last day (verse 39).
Every one which seeth the Son, and believeth on him, may have everlasting life; and I will raise him up at the last day (verse 40).
He that believeth on me hath everlasting life. I am that bread of life (verse 47, 48). If any man eat of this bread, he shall live forever (verse 51).

It could be assumed that in demonstration of this truth Lazarus was raised from his grave.[45]

The promise of everlasting life is not given unconditionally. Many of his own followers, hearing this discourse, left him and "walked no more with him" (John 6:66). Only believing on him is not enough: "If ye continue in my word, then are ye my disciples indeed."[46] The same is understood in the famous statement: "And this is life eternal, that they might know thee the only true God, and Jesus Christ, whom thou hast sent."[47] As he continues in this prayer, it is made clear that in addition to the knowledge of God and Jesus Christ there must be added the knowledge of the word (verses 6, 8, 14, and 20).

Jesus' teachings on eternal life brought charges against him before "the chief priests and all the council."[48] The actual statement made by Jesus was reported by John.[49] The occasion was the cleansing of the temple as the context shows. In verse 21, the author wants us to know that this reference was made regarding "the temple of his body," not the stone temple which took forty-seven years to build.

Hence, another dimension is added to the reason for the death of Jesus and the enrichment of human life. The early Christian church could not have succeeded in its ministry without the assurance of eternal life. Likewise, if the church today is to succeed in missionary and pastoral endeavors, eternal life must become a conviction, not a mere understanding.

Judgment

With man seen through the eyes of Jesus as a spiritual being possessing agency, and with life being eternal, one can readily understand his teachings on judgment. Without sin, eternal life, and judgment there would be no need or reason for redemption. Hence, in his Sermon on the Mount judgment on the sinner was identified with hell fire.[50] This was no isolated occasion but repeated over and over. "Fear not them which kill the body, but are not able to kill the soul; but rather fear him which is able to destroy both soul and body in hell."[51] He does not hesitate to speak of the worm that dieth not, and the fire that is not quenched.[52] Those who value life in terms of earthly goods only find themselves tormented with hell fire after death, while those who are apparently poor in material possessions but rich in their obedience toward God find themselves in eternal bliss (Abraham's bosom).[53] Those who thought that judgment was intended for others were warned to repent or they would "all likewise perish."[54] Of Judas he declared: "Good were it for that man if he had not been born."[55] He made no apology when he spoke of the "outer darkness" which engulfed the disobedient.[56] Neither did he hesitate to condemn the offender to be cast into the mighty deep with a millstone hanging around his neck.[57] Five of the ten virgins who were awaiting the wedding of the bridegroom were shut out of the festivity because they were unprepared.[58] Two of the three servants who were made stewards over their master's goods were rewarded favorably for their stewardship. The third, who buried the master's money, was thrown "into outer darkness" where there was "weeping and gnashing of teeth."[59] In the final judgment the sheep are to be separated from the goats. The first will be placed at the right hand of the judge, and he will say, "Inherit the kingdom prepared for you from the foundation of the world." The goats, placed at the left, will go to "everlasting fire, prepared for the devil and his angels."[60] The sheep were interested in caring for the just needs of unfortunate brethren, while the goats ignored these legitimate needs.

For those of us who shudder at the thought of hell fire and brimstone the symbolic aspect of this language should not be lost. If a man is a spirit, and so is God, then the judgment becomes a spiritual judgment.

If that man repenteth not, and remaineth and dieth an enemy to God, the demands of divine justice doth awaken his immortal soul to a lively sense of his own guilt, which doth cause him to shrink from the presence of the Lord, and doth fill his breast with guilt, and pain, and anguish, which is like an unquenchable fire, whose flames ascend up for ever and ever.[61]

DIRECT TEACHINGS OF JESUS

In view of the consecration prayer on the emblems which commits us to keep "his commandments," we may wonder what these commandments are. What we have already found of Jesus' teachings and examples in the first half of this chapter have been discovered through an indirect approach. Also it is difficult to recognize them as commandments and connect them with the Lord's Supper. Naturally, we may go to the great commandment: "Love the Lord thy God with all thy heart, and with all thy soul, and with all thy mind. . . and love thy neighbor as thyself,"[62] and let the case rest there. But this general approach needs defining. After all, murder has been justified, in some cases, on the ground of mercy. Ours is an age of rationalization. Any generalization which may come as a commandment can be easily rationalized in our complex society.

Even in his discourse on the Lord's Supper, found in the account according to John, the commandments were limited to love. Moses detailed his commandments and listed them in ten different categories. Even his ceremonial commandments were clearly defined. And when Paul spoke of love he had to divide it into its various aspects. Love "suffereth long, and is kind; charity envieth not; charity vaunteth not itself, is not puffed up, doth not behave itself unseemly, seeketh not her own, is not easily provoked, thinketh no evil."[63] If Moses and Paul went to great length explaining the commandments of God as they understood them, should not Jesus do the same? Indeed, he would be remiss in requiring us to keep his commandments without specifying and detailing what we need to observe. Fortunately, he did not leave us in a quandary. His commandments were plain and given at the first of his ministry as he appeared to the Nephites.

The Commandments of Jesus

The visit of Jesus on the Western Hemisphere was brief. In his message he dealt with the very essential. Where there was much debate between him and the Jews in the New Testament, there was no debate here. From the very beginning after his descent to the multitude, he designated the twelve disciples and began giving his commandments.[64] These preceded the enactment of the Lord's Supper, and are

209

the ones to be observed if the Eucharist is to be meaningful.

As we familiarize ourselves with these instructions we discover that we are reading the so-called "sermon on the mount" as recorded by Matthew. Familiarity has an unfortunate aspect—it breeds carelessness, which is what has happened in this case. Some reject the instruction on the ground that Joseph Smith simply copied the information from Matthew. By doing this, they reject the divine origin of the book. Others, knowing the sermon, do not connect it with the Lord's Supper. This is perhaps due to the long Christian heritage which regards the meal as a memorial of Jesus and excludes the "keeping of his commandments." After all, these words of commemoration are inscribed on many a table set for the observance of the meal. Nowhere on Christian pulpits (that I am aware of) is there an inscription of his commandments.

The Sermon Analyzed

Of the Synoptics only Matthew and Luke record the sermon. Mark, who (according to students) was the first to write the story of Jesus, does not mention it. Goodspeed, who argues for the authorship of Matthew by the apostle thus named, that in Mark there is no "sermon on the mount, no Lord's prayer, no beatitudes."[65] John does not mention it either. When the accounts of Matthew and Luke are compared, vital differences are found to exist between them. They differ in time, location, and the segment of the multitude to whom the message was addressed.

The Two Accounts Compared

Matthew's account was given at the very beginning

of Jesus' ministry. It was addressed to the multitude and the disciples.[66] The twelve were still ordinary followers. Their calling took place in the tenth chapter, while the sermon occupied the fifth through the seventh chapters. The place where it was given was on the mount.

Luke's account of the sermon is scattered over three chapters and is not continuous. Different incidents appear between each part of the sermon and the next, creating large gaps. The bulk of the discourse is found in the sixth chapter. The beatitudes are listed there but are fewer in number than those given by Matthew. The Lord's Prayer appears in the eleventh chapter and differs in wording from that recorded by Matthew. The instructions which Matthew lists in the sixth chapter, verses 25 ff, appear in Luke 12, verses 24-34 (22-31, K.J.). The message of those verses in Matthew is directed to the multitude. Luke singles them out to the twelve.

When time is considered, the sermon in Luke was given by Jesus after the twelve apostles were chosen. This is in direct opposition to Matthew's narrative. Luke also differs from Matthew on the location of the delivery. It was spoken on the plains after Jesus had come down from the mount.[67]

This brief comparison is necessary for those who reject the commandments of Jesus in the Book of Mormon on the ground that they are a copy of Matthew's sermon. They are not.

Nephi's Account

The wording of the sermon in the Book of Mormon is patterned mostly after Matthew's account. The substance, however, is vastly different. The probability exists that, since the information on the plates was so familiar to Joseph, he went ahead and used the wording of Matthew. At least it appears so on the surface. The audience, however, in the Book of Mormon was composed of the multitude and those chosen out of the multitude to become the twelve. Matthew's audience was made up of the multitude, with no twelve yet designated. Nephi's account gives the sermon the authority of a command: "For verily I say unto you, that except ye shall keep my commandments, which I have commanded you at this time, ye shall in no case enter into the kingdom of heaven."[68] Matthew's sermon, on the other hand, is simply instructive—"He . . . taught them."[69] If Matthew's chronology is followed, Jesus was not accepted as the Messiah until the twelve recognized him as "the Christ, the Son of the living God."[70] His identity was hidden from the multitude when he gave the sermon. He was thought of as a teacher, such as had risen on many occasions in the life of Israel. To the multitude on the Western Hemisphere he was the Christ, the one who descended to them after his resurrection from the grave in Palestine. For this reason his instruction to them carried a note of authority—the authority of the Son of God. The details of the sermon are "commandments" to be observed, not simply teachings.

Another vital departure in the American account is a break in the narrative where Jesus turned his attention from the multitude and addressed himself to the twelve disciples.[71] These verses correspond in wording to Matthew's (6:25 ff). As has been noted,

212

the Palestinian twelve had not yet been chosen. The twelve in Nephi's account were already "chosen to minister unto this people." In order to be freed from the cares of this life and magnify their calling, they had to depend on the heavenly Father. Here for the first time as I see it, is the inference for self-sustaining ministry.

Luke's Account Similar to Nephi's

Luke's account differs from Matthew's in chronology and in directing a portion of the discourse to the twelve. In this respect it is in agreement with Nephi's rendition, but it is addressed in such a subtle manner that it needs special attention.

This part of the sermon is found in Chapter 12. The gathering is composed of "an innumerable multitude of people" and the address is directed "unto his disciples first of all."[72] The conversation turns into a completely different subject beginning with verse 13. In verse 22, Jesus resumes his address to the "disciples." At this point we are left without any differentiation between one type of disciple and the other, but those who heard the address found it thought-provoking and disturbing. That this is so can be gathered from Peter's interruption as he asked, "Lord, speakest thou this parable unto us, or even to all?"

Since the audience was composed of innumerable people and the disciples, the "all" may be taken to include the whole gathering in spite of the fact that the disciples were singled out of the multitude. The complete text, however, does not allow us this liberty. That he was speaking to the disciples only is made implicit by the answer the Lord gave to

Peter: "Who then is that faithful and wise steward, whom his lord shall make ruler over his household, to give them their portion of meat in due season? Blessed is that servant, whom his lord when he cometh shall find so doing."[73] There were both the steward and the household; the whole gathering was not included. The household was the church (disciples) and the stewards were the twelve (also disciples) chosen to feed the household. Since the twelve were already chosen according to Luke, directing a special message to them was proper.[74]

Nephi's Contributions

Significance of these contributions should not be lost on us. To say that the commandments in the Book of Mormon account are copied from Matthew is not correct. The similarity is apparent only in wording. The direction of the message involves principles which stand at the very heart of the Christian message.

1. The first contribution which comes out of these comparisons is the question of historicity of the gospels. Already we have found harmonies between the Book of Mormon account of the Lord's Supper and the gospel of John. In my opinion this gospel has been proven to be a historical document written by John. This repeated harmony with the Nephite record may have contributed to the popular feeling that the Synoptic account grew out of tradition without any historical base. This feeling should now be dispelled by the discovery of the sermon in the Book of Mormon. Chronologically, Matthew and Luke's accounts differ; not so when Luke's account finds support in the

Nephites' record. Here we have a completely independent source, antedating biblical criticisms and directing part of the sermon to the twelve. If there are those who argue that Joseph Smith made the discovery of Luke's account and imitated it by directing that part of the message to the twelve as he wrote the Book of Mormon, they are immediately confronted with wording. Luke's words do not appear in Nephi's account. Logically, we have to come to the conclusion that Nephi's account is independent of both and contributes in no small measure to the historicity of the sermon, though some variations entered into the Synoptics.

2. The historical harmony between Luke and Nephi should assist in the solution of the prolonged debate between Catholics who adhere to a specially called and ordained priesthood and the Protestants who believe in the priesthood of all believers. The debate has been fruitless so far. That there were apostles in the Christian church in Palestine is fully recognized by both groups. The apostolic witness was established also by Jesus as he visited the Nephites. The intriguing factor, however, is Luke's connection of the steward (twelve) with the coming of the Lord in judgment.[75] This is an unmistakably eschatological note which can't be ignored.[76] According to Luke there will be twelve apostles in the church before the coming of the Lord as there were both in Palestine and the Americas. It is interesting that Joseph's decision to have twelve in the church was patterned after the Book of Mormon account, not the New Testament.[77] Thus, for those who accept the divine origin of the Book of Mormon, the debate is settled

by this independent evidence. Priesthood in the church is intended to be continuous—such as God set some in the primitive church to be apostles, prophets, and teachers,[78] and such as the apostle left Titus in Crete to set in order and ordain elders in every city.[79] The church which was created by the Lord as he visited the other sheep on the Americas has the same privilege of receiving from God and ordaining men to the priesthood.

3. The most important factor of this discussion is the divinity of the commandments of Jesus. Anyone seriously participating in the celebration of the Lord's Supper after respecting the illumination given to the meal by Nephi cannot ignore the fact that the Eucharist is a commemoration of Jesus' suffering as well as a commemoration of his commandments. Jesus is not simply the teacher that Matthew's Sermon on the Mount makes him. His Messiahship was recognized by his disciples according to Luke's account, and the Book of Mormon confirms this. In addition, the Book of Mormon account calls the sermon "Commandments." Without them there can be no proper celebration of the Lord's Supper.

The Covenant Is Made More Meaningful

It is at this juncture more than at any other previous reference to it that the covenant is made meaningful and operative. To enter into a covenant with no instruction to abide by and no provisions made to enable one to carry out the promises made is not covenanting at all. The word becomes an empty statement carrying neither rewards nor penalties. The promissory obligations are absent, or—if we should consider the Sermon on the Mount to be the standard the Lord wants us to live by as we celebrate his Supper—the instructions in both Matthew and Luke have no connection with the sacred meal. Observance of its precepts becomes optional. A different story would have appeared had the instructions either preceded or followed the institution of the Supper, but this is not the case. Left as it is, the Lord's Supper account in the New Testament is ill-defined, and students of both open and close Communion can draw misty conclusions supporting their differing views. After all, the common notion is that the Lord's Supper is a memorial of Jesus only. This is not so, however, when John's account of the meal is combined with that of the Book of Mormon. Here the words, commandments, and teachings of Jesus are inseparably linked to his person.

In the waters of baptism, we are granted salvation on the grounds that we are committed to the observance of the commandments of Jesus. When the priest petitions God for the congregation to "always remember him [Jesus] and keep his commandments" the covenanting worshipers hark back to their own baptism. There they committed themselves to God and to these precepts. It is this petition that stirs the serious soul for self-examination. Where infraction of these commandments has taken place the covenanting servant, through repentance, makes new resolves. The inward spiritual qualifications make one fit for the kingdom of God. Under the rest of what we have become accustomed to calling the Sermon on the Mount, we find a long list of behavioral activities we should observe. These involve our responsibility to God and to our fellowmen.

217

Provisions Made for Compliance

It is often heard that in the Sermon on the Mount the teachings of Jesus are summed up in a beautiful manner. This is true, but when it comes to their practical application in life, people become apologetic and consider them simply as ideals. Jesus did not entertain such a notion though he recognized the fact that "the spirit is indeed willing; but the flesh is weak."[80] It is now becoming clearer that Jesus' purpose in instituting the Lord's Supper was not only to establish a memorial for himself but also to provide a practical way by which the teachings he lived and died for could be observed by his disciples.

When the priest petitions God that the participants may "keep his commandments," he is not asking that they be kept just as ideals. As Jesus discoursed with the twelve in Jerusalem when the Supper was first instituted, he gave them this instruction: "If ye keep my commandments, ye shall abide in my love; even as I have kept my Father's commandments, ye shall abide in my love; even as I have kept my Father's commandments, and abide in his love."[81] Jesus did not consider these commandments as mere ideals. His literal application of them led him to the cross. But the statements in Matthew's account which caused students to feel that in some cases Jesus was speaking idealistically are absent from the account in the Book of Mormon.[82] No one is asked to pluck an eye or amputate a hand in case these parts of his body lead him to an offense. Neither can Joseph Smith be accused of manipulating the text to arrive at the conclusion that these commandments are not to be practically observed. Had he done so, change should also have been made in the language of the Inspired Version. That text follows Matthew's rendition.

It is significant that when Jesus appeared to the Nephites and introduced himself, he said, "I have suffered the will of the Father in all things, from the beginning."[83] Without suffering, Jesus could not have accomplished the will of God and kept his precepts. Neither can limited Zion nor the universal kingdom of God become reality without suffering. This appears to be the major reason for tying the commandments of Jesus to the Lord's Supper and associating both—the commandments and Jesus—with suffering. Whether we like it or not, suffering is an unavoidable part of life. Peter recognized this fact when he admonished the saints of his day, "For it is better, if the will of God be so, that ye suffer for well doing, than for evil doing."[84] If the church is not to suffer by applying the teachings of Jesus in our earthly life and by building his kingdom, we will suffer through wars, depressions, recessions, rebellion, civil strife, class struggle, division in the home, dishonesty in government, mugging and raping on the street, and international dislocations at a time when men are armed with instruments of destruction which threaten the survival of the human species.

The example and teachings of Jesus symbolized by the bread and wine are called the body and blood of Jesus. In them the covenanting individual sees a checklist of commandments made practical in life against which he measures his attitude and conduct. Where compliance has been lacking, regardless of how difficult he finds it to comply, with prayer and the

219

Lord's example he will resolve to do better in the future. By such participation in the sacred meal he will be building "a house on the rock." This is the "going on to perfection" of which the writer to the Hebrews speaks.[85]

It is the linking of the commandments of Jesus to the Lord's Supper in the prayer of consecration which compels the church to observe close Communion. Removal of this linkage will gradually lead to nihilism, the process of which we may be the present unconscious observers.

1. John 15:10.
2. Dean M. Kelly, *Why Conservative Churches Are Growing*, Harper and Row, 1972. Kelly's argument is disputed but his conclusion is sound.
3. II Corinthians 5:21.
4. Mark 14:43.
5. Matthew 10:25.
6. Genesis 2:8.
7. Deuteronomy 32:5, 6.
8. John 1:12, 13.
9. John 4:25.
10. John 8:41, 44.
11. Matthew 12:10.
12. Luke 15:8-10.
13. Luke 15:11 ff.
14. Mark 2:27.
15. John 5:10-16.
16. Matthew 6:24.
17. Matthew 22:17-21.
18. Matthew 6:22, 23.
19. Luke 12:15-23.
20. Matthew 16:29.
21. Matthew 5:30.
22. John 8:3-11.
23. Matthew 15:18.
24. Matthew 9:11-14.
25. Matthew 5:10.
26. Matthew 12:24, 38-39; Luke 11:25-27.
27. John 12:31.
28. John 8:44.

29. Matthew 8:9, 10; Luke 7:1-10.
30. Matthew 15:20-27; Mark 7:22-29.
31. Luke 4:16-30.
32. Genesis 37:35; 42:38; I Samuel 2:6.
33. Job 14:14, 19:26.
34. Matthew 19:16; Mark 10:15; Luke 18:18.
35. Luke 10:26
36. Matthew 19:23 ff.
37. Matthew 21:45.
38. John 3:3, 5.
39. John 1:4, K.J.
40. John 14:6; 6:40.
41. John 3:36, K.J.
42. John 5:24, 28, 29.
43. Matthew 19:27-29; Mark 10:28-30; Luke 18:28-30.
44. John 4:16.
45. John 11:1-45.
46. John 8:31.
47. John 17:3.
48. Mark 14:60-69.
49. John 2:19-21.
50. Matthew 5:24, 32, 33.
51. Matthew 10:25.
52. Mark 9:41, 43, 48.
53. Luke 16:24-30.
54. Luke 13:1-5.
55. Matthew 26:20.
56. Matthew 8:12; 22:13.
57. Matthew 18:6; Mark 9:42; Luke 17:2.
58. Matthew 25:1-11.
59. Matthew 25:14-30.
60. Matthew 25:31 ff.
61. Mosiah 1:83, 84.
62. Mark 12:34-36.
63. I Corinthians 13:4, 5.
64. III Nephi 5:17-7:11.
65. Edgar J. Goodspeed, *Matthew, Apostle and Evangelist*, Winston, Philadelphia, 1959, p. 104.
66. Matthew 5:1; Luke 6:17.
67. Luke 6:12-17.
68. III Nephi 5:68.
69. Matthew 5:2.
70. Matthew 16:14-17.
71. III Nephi 6:3-12.
72. Luke 12:1.
73. Luke 12:42, 43, K.J.
74. Luke 6:13-16.
75. Luke 12:54-57.

76. Luke 12:39-42.
77. Doctrine and Covenants 16.
78. I Corinthians 12:28.
79. Titus 1:5.
80. Matthew 26:38.
81. Jonah 15:10.
82. Matthew 5:32, 33.
83. III Nephi 5:12.
84. I Peter 3:17.
85. Hebrews 6:1.

CHAPTER EIGHT

JESUS RISEN AND GLORIFIED

All I have said in the previous chapters is empty rhetoric without the resurrection. Remove the bodily resurrection of the Lord from the New Testament account and Jesus becomes a moralist in his social teachings and a speculator about eternal life. There are two reasons for doubt in the resurrection of the body: the confusing account of the evangelists on the subject, and the lack of belief in a miracle of this nature.

I shall not attempt in this study to add to or subtract from the debate which has been going on for a century and a half. Indeed, it would be presumptuous of me to do so. The ground has been covered by devout men who are much more qualified to deal with the question than I am. What we shall do here is study the resurrection account in the New Testament and discover the harmonies and the contradictions between the evangelists. This will be done with the hope that the new revelation of Christ to the Nephites may shed light on the problem and assist us in observing the Lord's Supper as Jesus intended us to do. After all, the bread we eat and the wine we drink are symbols of the

223

body of Christ. Was Jesus crucified in vain, or did he arise from the grave as we are told? If in vain, then the Lord's Supper becomes a social meal in memory of a good man. But if we discover the resurrection to be a fact, then we will be giving ourselves unreservedly for the imitation of his example and the observance of his teachings.

The New Testament Account

Matthew's account of the resurrection is the most descriptive.[1] He wrote of the two Marys, the securely sealed tomb, and the guard. According to him an earthquake took place and two angels came down from heaven, rolled away the stone which sealed the tomb, and sat on it. The watchmen were terrified and shook with fear. The angels turned and said to the two women: "Fear not ye; for we know that ye seek Jesus who was crucified. He is not here; for he is risen." Then the angels asked them to see the empty grave where they had laid Jesus. They also instructed the women to go and tell the disciples that Jesus would meet them in Galilee. As the women were on their way back Jesus appeared to them and repeated what the angels had instructed them to do. Then the watchmen who were guarding the tomb revealed to the Jewish leaders what had happened. The leaders bribed the watchmen and told them to say his disciples came and stole the body while they were asleep. The eleven disciples went to Galilee, apparently to a previously arranged place, where Jesus appeared to them and gave them the great commission.

Mark's account is brief and differs considerably

from Matthew's.[2] In it he tells of three women going to the tomb instead of two. They bought spices to anoint Christ's body, but on the way they wondered how they could roll away the stone. When they arrived at the tomb, however, they found that the great stone already had been removed. As they entered the sepulcher they saw angels who told them not to fear because "Jesus is risen." As in Matthew's account, the angels showed them the place where Christ had been laid and instructed them to tell the disciples and Peter to go to Galilee for the meeting with Jesus. Then the narrative abruptly ends. Unlike Matthew, Mark does not mention an earthquake.

The major stumbling block in this narrative is this quick ending. If the resurrection mentioned was a historical physical resurrection, Mark did not tell of any later appearance of Jesus. The oldest manuscript available ends Chapter 16 with verse 8 and the words, "for they were afraid." Verses 9 to 20 which follow in the King James account are of a later insertion—some think "not earlier than the fourth century of our era."[3] This abrupt ending of the account was the subject of heated debate among students. Since the appearance of the Standard Revised Version and the New English Bible the laymen can join in the argument. Both of these versions omit verses 9 ff.

One may accept the King James account with the later insertion, or take the new ending with verse 8. Then there is a third choice. One ancient manuscript adds these words after verse 8:

But they reported briefly to Peter and those with him all that they had been told. And after this, Jesus himself sent out by means of them, from east to west, the sacred and imperishable proclamation of eternal salvation.

It may be noticed from this that only the doctored-up King James account tells of a physical resurrection and appearance.[4] Regardless of what the critics say or new authorities disclose, the tomb was still empty. Another but lesser problem faces the skeptic—the purchase of spices. The women were Jews in a totally Jewish city, and the occasion was the Feast of the Passover. No stores were allowed open. Where did they purchase the spices?

Luke's narrative is longer than the preceding two and similar to them in the account of the empty tomb.[5] Differences after this increase. Instead of two or three women going to the tomb, Luke mentioned many. Also instead of one angel (as reported in the King James version) addressing the women he had two with "shining garments" announcing the joyous news: "Why seek ye the living among the dead? He is not here, but is risen." After this he reminded them of the prediction Jesus made to them in Galilee regarding his suffering, crucifixion, and resurrection on the third day, and they remembered it. The women then returned and related the story to the apostles, but "their words seemed to them as idle tales, and they believed them not." Then Peter went to the sepulcher and verified the story for himself—with wonderment.

Right at this point a break appears in Luke's story as he introduces the narrative of the two men bound for Emmaus. Jesus appeared to the men and visited with them. Then—since it was evening—they invited him to abide with them. Subject of the conversation was the story the women told of the disappearance of Jesus and the empty tomb. As bread was broken for the evening meal they recognized

226

that the stranger was Jesus. They arose after he disappeared from their midst and went back to Jerusalem and told their story. As they were telling of their unique experience, Jesus appeared and said to them, "Peace be unto you." The people were terrified. They thought they had seen a spirit. Knowing their thoughts, Jesus assured them, saying that a spirit had no flesh and bones; then he bade them to handle him. Following this he asked for food, and they gave him a piece of broiled fish and honey. He ate the meal before them. In all of this Luke appears to be combating the idea that the story of the resurrection was only a spiritual vision or imagination.

Beautiful as this story is, aside from minor disagreements with the previous two writers, it has aroused considerable debate and suspicion. Instead of Jesus appearing in Galilee, as recorded in the preceding accounts, Luke wrote of his appearance in Jerusalem.

John's account of the resurrection is still different from the other three accounts. It is recorded in two chapters,[6] but students agree that 21 is of later addition. John wrote of Mary Magdalene going to the tomb not at sunrise but while it was yet dark. Here there was only one woman instead of the two in Matthew, three in Mark, and many in Luke. When the stone was removed from the sepulcher the body was not there. Then Magdalene told Peter and the beloved disciple, and they ran to the sepulcher. They verified her story and went home, but she stood there grieving. When she looked again in the sepulcher she found two angels in white—one at the head the the other at the feet of where Jesus had lain. When they asked her why she was weeping she told them that the Lord had been taken away and she did not know where he had been laid. Then she happened to look around and saw Jesus, but she supposed him to be the gardener. When he called her by name, however, she immediately recognized him. She was bidden not to touch him but rather to go and give the disciples this message: "I ascend unto my Father, and your Father."

That same evening, while the doors were shut, Jesus appeared to the disciples and said, "Peace be unto you." With that he showed them his pierced hands and side. Thomas was not there and did not believe what he was told. The following week Jesus appeared again to the disciples, and Thomas was present. He was told to touch Jesus' hands and side "and be not faithless, but believing." These two appearances took place in Jerusalem, not in Galilee. John also recorded a third appearance—at the sea of Tiberias.

This does not solve the problem of Galilee or Jerusalem, however. The twenty-first chapter, according to the critics, is of doubtful origin. So Jesus appeared in Jerusalem, as Luke stated, and in Galilee, as Matthew and Mark recorded. Apparently the scribe who edited John added the last chapter in order to bridge the gap between the Matthew and Luke accounts—at least this is the reasoning of some critics.

When the stories of the four evangelists are compared, vast differences appear. Matthew is discredited outright as a historian because of the mistake he makes relative to Judas' betrayal.[7] He attributes the whole episode to a prophecy uttered by Jeremy the prophet, while in reality the prophecy is found in Zechariah.[8] If he is wrong in his citation of a reference, he can't be relied on in case of the resurrection. Mark's account is inconclusive, especially when he is considered to have written his gospel before the other three. Luke adds the Emmaus story which finds no parallel among the other three accounts. John's gospel is considered by critics to have been written in the second century and "doctored" by the insertion of the bridging of the gap between Jerusalem and Galilee.

Defenders of the bodily resurrection account found a harmony in this diversity which the radical critic had to admit: in all the four accounts there is an agreement on the empty tomb.

Paul's Testimony

The strongest evidence of a bodily resurrection comes from Paul, but his testimony is not without challenge. What makes it significant is its age. It appeared before the tradition of the gospel account was written. Its advocates figure that the death of the Lord took place in A.D. 29 or 30. Paul's conversion took place in A.D. 30, and his letter to the Corinthians was written in A.D. 53. His visit to Peter in Jerusalem is placed in 33, making a difference of twenty years between the visit and the time of writing. Thus his testimony is firsthand testimony and not spoiled by the passage of time. His letter is addressed to believers who came into the church through his own preaching. Its purpose is to remind them

that Christ died for our sins according to the scriptures; and

229

that he was buried, and that he rose again the third day
according to the scriptures; and that he was seen of Cephas,
then of the twelve; after that, he was seen of about five
hundred brethren at once; of whom the greater part remain
unto this present, but some are fallen asleep. After that, he was
seen of James, then of all the apostles. And last of all he was
seen of me also, as of one born out of due time.[9]

The emphasis of the statement is placed on the
word "seen." This company saw Jesus after he arose
from the grave. Paul then adds his own testimony
by saying, "He was seen of me also." This occurred
the same year the Lord arose from the grave, when
Paul was on his way to Damascus to persecute the
infant group. The story of his conversion is recorded
by Luke three times in the book of Acts.[10] There
is slight difference in the way he tells the experience,
but in all three he speaks of a sensory experience
completely outside himself: he heard, he saw, was
stricken to the ground, and was made temporarily
blind. From the time of his ordination until his
imprisonment in Rome his preaching, according to
Luke, centered on the resurrection of the Lord.[11]

Clear as his testimony is, it is not convincing
to the critics. What bothers them is his explanation
of how the dead will rise:[12]

That which thou sowest, thou sowest not that body that shall
be, but grain, it may be of wheat, or some other; but God
giveth it a body as it hath pleased him.

This is in contradiction to Jewish teachings of the
time which were based on belief in a complete
resurrection of the material body. When verse 44
is added to this the result is a conflict—the spiritual
body as against the physical.

Some students take shelter under two statements
Paul makes in his second letter to the Corinthians,

230

feeling that he changed his mind on the subject, or at least became confused. The first appears to substitute immortality in heaven for the resurrection.[13] The second regards his visions and revelations of which he does not appear to be sure.[14]

Differing Theories

It is natural that out of the confusing resurrection accounts different interpretations should arise. The oldest are the fainting and theft theories. Those who support the first speculate that since Jesus was not long on the cross he did not die; he only fainted. After being taken down, he revived. The other is based on the idea that his disciples stole him away. Both of these have lost their appeal. The dominant theories now are psychological. One is the meditative idea. The disciples reflected on his person and teaching for such a long time that ultimately they saw visions of him. This psychological reflection was then transferred from mind to sight. But since this would have taken an extended period of time, some students reject it in favor of the sudden-excitement theory. None of the disciples, they argue, witnessed the suffering, crucifixion, and burial of the Lord. In an atmosphere like this they could imagine him as still alive, and the imagination coupled with excitement over his enduring teachings would produce visions of his continued presence. Others who believe in the vision theory attribute the visions to God and Christ. These divinely given manifestations resulted in the belief that he was still alive. Their final conclusion dismisses the objective fact of the resurrection. The whole question then rests on the grounds of subjectivity, which believers in the Book of Mormon have compelling reasons to reject.

The Account of the Book of Mormon

The Book of Mormon has one central theme—the divinity of Jesus. It claims three important facts which need verification. First, there was a migration of Israelitish people from Palestine to the Americas. Second, there was among the migrants prophetic insight regarding the coming of the Messiah in the flesh to the Jews and his visitation to the Nephites in the Western Hemisphere after his resurrection from the tomb in Jerusalem. Third, there was his descent on the Nephites, in the flesh, and his subsequent ministry.

It is felt that in the course of this study these three features of the book have already been justified. But in order to refresh our minds and approach the subject of the resurrection with an unbiased attitude, I shall briefly review our discoveries.

1. *The presence of Israelitish people on the Americas.* There were speculations at the time the Book of Mormon was written that the Indians were of Israelitish origin. The Book of Mormon account rests not on speculation but on verified facts:

a. How can one account for the presence of the doctrine of baptism *as a covenant* in the Book of Mormon when the idea was completely foreign to the Christian world of the time, and later on—after the publication of the book—was found to have been a doctrine among Jews years before Christ and was administered to proselytes, unless there had existed a common source of knowledge between the two separated groups? (See page 126.)

b. How can we account for a Joseph legend in the Book of Mormon when the knowledge of such a legend was hidden from the world until unearthed by Schonfield and published in 1965 without a common origin before the separation of the principals?

c. How can one account for the presence in the Book of Mormon of the creation of good and evil inclinations in man when such an idea did not exist in the world of Joseph Smith (and especially his locality) but later on was discovered to have been among the Jews before the advent of the Lord, unless the idea was brought with the migrants about 600 years before Christ? (See page 176.)

I have selected these three points because I feel they are sufficiently convincing that a migration from Palestine to the Americas took place—as the Book of Mormon states—under the leadership and guidance of the heavenly Father.

2. *The question of pre-Christ Christology.* Although this appears anachronistic to some, it is upheld by the endowment of a special spiritual insight to the descendants of Joseph (see pages 185-192). In their state of isolation they were particularly blessed with spiritual manifestations pointing to their redemption through the atonement of Christ (pages 168-170). Interestingly, the word "ransom"—which has discredited the subject of atonement—is absent from their literature.

3. *Descent to the Nephites.* The preceding review brings us back into a position where we can consider the resurrection. Since there were "other sheep," as we have discovered, the comment of Jesus as reported

by John regarding them is a bona fide statement.[15] Commentators have puzzled over it and now seem to ignore it. At first it was explained that these sheep were the gentile nations. But in weighing the question against other New Testament statements on the subject, students discovered that the mission of Jesus at his first advent was limited only to the house of Israel.[16] When the twelve were called and ordained, their mission excluded the gentiles and Samaritans.[17] This left the identity of the other sheep in question.

Since the coming of the Book of Mormon the story has changed. As we have already found out, God led a portion of the house of Israel, of the seed of Joseph, to the Americas. In turn, this has solved the question of the resurrection of Jesus. His promise that the "other sheep" would hear his voice has been fulfilled. After his resurrection from the grave in Jerusalem he appeared physically and ministered to the Nephites. Those who may be tempted to argue that Joseph Smith, knowing of John's reference to the other sheep, seized on the idea and contrived a visitation of Jesus to the Nephites, are under the necessity of explaining how practices and beliefs among the Jews prior to the Christian era happened to appear in the Book of Mormon.

Jesus Glorified

The glorification of Jesus provides us with another evidence of his resurrection and appearing to the other or lost sheep. As Jesus descends on the multitude on this hemisphere, he is introduced by these words which appear only in the gospel according to John: "Behold, my beloved Son, in whom I am well pleased, in whom I have glorified my name, hear ye him."[18] And then Christ says: "I am the light and the life of the world, . . . and have glorified the Father in taking upon me the sins of the world."[19] The presence of the word "glorified" in both the introduction and the response reminds us again of the similarity of Book of Mormon language to that of John.[20]

The background for John's account is found in the preceding verses of the chapter. The news of the raising of Lazarus had spread rapidly. The occasion was six days before the Passover when Jerusalem was filled with foreigners coming for the celebration. They gathered to see the miracle performer. It was an hour of great triumph for Jesus. In spite of that, he was troubled. The time of his suffering and death was approaching. Out of his anguished soul he cried: "Father, glorify thy name." Then there came a voice from heaven: "I have glorified it, and will glorify it again." The emphasis in this case was on the "glorify it again." Past glorification was accomplished by the miraculous voice which was heard by Jesus and the multitude. Some people thought they heard thunder, while others thought an angel spoke to Jesus. This voice must also have confirmed to them the news regarding the raising of Lazarus. But what about the future glorification promised by the voice? Jesus prayed for such glorification later on,[21] but no answer was given, no voice was heard.

Could it be that the promised glorification took place as Jesus descended to the waiting multitude in America? The strong probability is that it did. But the fact cannot be dismissed that the bodily resurrection of Jesus was also the promised glorification. This may sound like double talk, but it is not. When Jesus spoke of the other sheep hearing his voice, he was speaking of two groups of Israelites— one was hearing it in Palestine, and the other was yet to hear it in the Americas. If the Father's name was to be glorified it should be glorified to both, and it was. To the believers of the Jews the Father's name was glorified in the resurrection of Jesus from the tomb. And to the lost sheep the Father's name was glorified in both the resurrection and his descent to them. There could have been no descent without the resurrection, and the resurrection account in the New Testament would be lacking (as it surely is) without the evidence of the personal presence of Jesus among the Nephites.

There is no attempt in the Book of Mormon to correct the New Testament account of the resurrection—no answer to the problem of how many women went to the tomb, how many angels appeared on the scene, how the spices were bought on the most sacred of the Jewish holy days, and whether Jesus appeared in Jerusalem, Galilee, or both. Neither is there a reason given as to why the earliest of Mark's manuscripts ends Chapter 16 with verse 8. This is as it should be.

The account of the Book of Mormon is not to correct but rather to bear witness of the appearance, personal presence, and ministry of Jesus to the Nephites after his resurrection. The confusing factor in the New Testament account is that, with the exception of John, none of the authors who wrote a history of Jesus' ministry were eyewitnesses. They depended on the transmitted oral word. Regardless of these differences, however, one should not ignore their total agreement on the empty tomb. Since the fainting and theft theories are being discarded, the answer given by John remains. After the Lord vacated the tomb and gave evidence of his resurrection to his followers by even eating with them in Palestine, he appeared and ministered to the lost sheep of the house of Israel in America. By these two closely related acts, the Palestinian resurrection and the American appearance, the names of the Father and Son were glorified. (The name of Father and Son are glorified now, in our day, by virtue of their self-disclosure to humanity in the Book of Mormon. God is not dead, and Jesus is the Christ.)

Future Declaration of the Father's Name

Another evidence supporting the resurrection of Jesus is found in a short statement of his: "I have declared unto them thy name, and will declare it" (John 17:26). This chapter, which contains his farewell prayer, ends the instruction to the twelve and concludes the activity of the Lord's Supper. In a few moments Jesus' betrayal, trial, and death were to take place. Why the declaration of the Father's name when his mission on earth was practically ended? What else could he say in this short time that he was not able to say before? The natural and easy answer would be, "His death and resurrection." But this appears insufficient when his whole mission is carefully considered.

In making this statement Jesus has a definite purpose in mind. Understanding it depends on understanding his mission as recorded by John. Once this is done we will return to this chapter and explore the purposes toward which the prayer is directed.

The Mission of Jesus

In order to understand this mission as recorded in the tenth chapter of John we must study the whole chapter. The occasion was the Feast of Dedication (verse 22). A dispute arose between the Jews and Jesus. It appears certain that his claim to be the Shepherd of Israel and all that is connected with it precipitated the hostility. This claim had a much deeper meaning to his audience than is generally conceived. The only Shepherd of Israel the Jews knew of was God:

> Behold, the Lord God will come with strong hand, and his arm shall rule for him; behold, his reward is with him, and his work before him. He shall feed his flock like a shepherd; he shall gather the lambs with his arm, and carry them in his bosom, and shall gently lead those that are with young.—Isaiah 40:10, 11.

The Jews were divided after hearing this claim (verse 19). Some saw in Jesus the fulfillment of Isaiah's prophecy, and naturally some had different views. What may have increased the confusion is not only Jesus' claim to be the Shepherd of Israel but the additional claim of gathering the other scattered sheep into the fold of God. This assumption brought to their minds another prophecy spoken by Ezekiel:

> For thus saith the Lord God; Behold, I, even I, will both search my sheep, and seek them out. As a shepherd seeketh out his flock in the day that he is among his sheep that are scattered; so will I seek out my sheep, and will deliver them out of the places where they have been scattered in the cloudy and dark day.—Ezekiel 34:11, 12.

To those who believed in Jesus this statement was a

fulfillment of a divine promise. He was to gather the scattered flock of Israel and make one undivided fold. But many were skeptical. The claim he made was Messianic. That is why they said· "How long dost thou make us to doubt? If thou be the Christ, tell us plainly" (verse 24). No one can ignore their perplexity, but it appears that when he said, "I and my father are one" (verse 30) the simmering issue came to a head. He made himself equal with God. Such a statement was blasphemous and, according to the law, called for stoning (Leviticus 24:26). In his defense Jesus said, "Say ye of him, whom the Father hath sanctified, and sent into the world, Thou blasphemest; because I said, I am the son of God?" (verse 36). In this verse we see the mission of Jesus. The Father had sanctified him for a world mission with his personal activity centered on the Jews and scattered Israel. (The word "sanctified" in the Revised Standard version is rendered "consecrated," which is the meaning Jesus had in mind.) If we focus on this we can better understand the need for future declaration of the Father's name.

Jesus' Farewell Prayer

Since the future declaration is found in the last verse of this prayer, a study of Chapter 17 is necessary for background on the statement. This chapter is unique in gospel literature and hides more meaning for our mission than can be discussed here. Out of the comparison of the consecration prayer of the twelve found in it with the consecration prayer of the emblems found in the Book of Mormon, the mystery of Justin Martyr's lost prayer which Jesus taught was solved. A similar clarification awaits us

239

now as we consider the need for further declaration of the Father's name.

This prayer is pronounced for three differing purposes. The first eight verses are a prayer of thanksgiving. The hour Jesus has been awaiting has at last come (verse 1). Special notice should be given to John's purpose in reference to the hour of Jesus. At the marriage feast in Cana, Jesus told his mother, "Mine hour is not yet come" (2:4). When the Jews sought his life but abstained from killing him John said it was "because his hour was not yet come" (7:30; 8:20). According to John's narrative, when Jesus serves the Lord's Supper, he knows that his hour has come (13:1). The same is repeated in the first verse of this prayer. In this short period of time, Jesus declares the name of the Father in a very convincing manner which is to serve for ages to come. The twelve are now ready. They believe that Jesus came from God and that his message is divine. There is perfect unity among the three, and they understand their mission. Eternal life is now secure in the knowledge that Jesus and the Father are one.

The second division is found in verses 9 through 19. Here he prays for the twelve and their future mission. As he was consecrated and sent into the world, the twelve are now so consecrated (verse 19).

The third prayer is directed to the church which will be created by the activities of the twelve and their successors. This leads us to the last verse and the future declaration of the Father's name.

Why the Name?

The teachings of Jesus appear to have been perplexing to his audiences. Nicodemus was mystified by his message. The Sanhedrin was divided on his claims. Many of his followers left him when they heard his discourse connecting the living bread with his person. He was about to be stoned when he denounced as thieves and robbers all who came before him and declared himself to be the only true Shepherd of Israel and the Son of God. Even his inner circle, the twelve, would soon forsake him in the hour of his greatest need. Jesus was not ignorant of this. What is at stake here is the name of the Father who commissioned him. In whose name does he come? When Moses inquired of the identity of the one addressing him from the burning bush, he was told: "I am that I am." Later on the Jews gave the name of God as Yahweh. Subsequently, Jewish tradition, out of respect to God, forbade mention of Yahweh and simply used the "name." Throughout the gospels the name of God is given as the Father. John uses this nearly fifty times, and in most cases it is connected with the Son and his mission. Then the name of the Father is given as love. "God so loved" was the keynote of John's message. In reality this is rhetorical abstraction. In the coming hour Jesus would demonstrate the name of God, his relationship to the Father, and give eternal life a visible reality that could not be duplicated in mere words. In this period of time, starting with Calvary and ending with the resurrection, the love of God was to become manifested to all humanity.

The Triple Action of the Hour of Jesus

First, the apostles seized on the tragedy and triumph of Jesus and consecrated themselves by sharing his love with the world. The best example of this consecration is Luke's account in Acts. It is here we see the best example of their dedication to the message Jesus taught them. The choice before them was martyrdom or compromise. They chose to die—not because they despaired of life but because the message they carried was the gospel of love, the eternal truth. The epistles breathe the same story. Even the others who followed the twelve suffered the same fate. They struggled against false teachers, declared the saving message in the face of opposition (both from the Jews and the empire), and assembled the written gospel. Though it is not perfect, as we have already discovered, this written word has served the church and the cause of the Lord until our times.

During this same period of success, however, signs of decay began to appear in the church. Jesus made this significant statement in his Lord's Supper discourse: "Hereafter I will not talk much with you: for the prince of this world cometh, and hath nothing in me" (14:30, K.J.). The Revised Standard Version renders this "He has no power over me." There is a veiled warning in this statement. Though this prince has no power over Christ, the others were to be careful lest he overpower them. This is made clear in 17:15. Paul was aware of this when he warned the Ephesian church: "For we wrestle not against flesh and blood, but against principalities, against powers, against the rulers of the darkness of this world" (6:12). The church's struggle against Gnosticism, early controversies, dependence on imperial power, divisions which followed the political division of the empire, the dogmatic and dictatorial stand which led to protests and divisions, and finally the divisions of the protesters speak eloquently of the conquest of the evil one. Worse than this is the recent discovery that the gospel record is not as sound as it is supposed to be. All of this makes the hour on which Jesus depended so much to announce his future declaration appear to have been a complete failure. But such is not so when we consider the second "action" of the declaration concerning the scattered sheep. For this objective Jesus was nearly stoned. Also, he came to conquer, not to be conquered. He conquered the evil one but had reservation on the ability of the church to conquer. He prayed that the faithful might be protected from evil, and in John 16:33 they were told of the tribulation they would have in this world. He finished by saying, "be of good cheer, I have overcome the world." The church was badly overcome, and the written gospel on which it depended appeared to be lacking in clarity. How could Jesus rescue that which was lost and bring victory out of defeat?

Jesus' mission to the scattered sheep is highly confusing. The only parallel to this statement of John in, the Synoptic account is found in Matthew 15:23: "I am not sent but unto the lost sheep of the house of Israel." To me this pronouncement appears final. I may clarify my feelings by saying that his personal mission in the flesh was limited to Israel. After some harsh protests he healed the Canaanite girl and answered the plea of the centurion (Matthew 8:5), but his main mission was the lost sheep of Israel. Commentators differ widely on the meaning of this statement by Matthew, and such is to be expected. Only half of the story appears here.

Defeat was turned into victory as Jesus visited the scattered sheep of Israel who were brought to the Americas. The Western Hemisphere, as far as our knowledge goes, was not known to the Jews of Jesus' day; neither did they appear to have had a clear conception of where the tribes were scattered. Had Jesus told them, his case would have been worsened. There is no need for us to refer back to evidences we have discovered in this study supporting their migration to this land. There is need, however, to know that their guidance to this land and Christ's visit to them was the strategy the Lord used to gather them into the main fold and conquer the evil which brought darkness to the church. The resurrection of Jesus was the step taken to bring them to the fold of God. Through his presence among the lost sheep the gospel was planted in the Americas as it was established in Palestine. Without the bodily resurrection of Jesus we would have had no gospel and would not have heard of any lost sheep.

The Significance of Timing

Throughout the Old and New Testaments the timing of events appears to be important. Its value is mentioned in Ecclesiastes 3:1-8, and Daniel echoes the same thing as he points to future events (7:22; 11:40). We have already discovered the timing element concerning the "hour of Jesus." In Acts 3:21 we read of a future time of refreshing. Paul speaks of the fullness of the times of the Gentiles (Romans 11:25) and later writes of the dispensation of the fullness of times (Ephesians 1:10). I also made this clear in my *Insight into the Book of Revelation*. This is brought out to show how important timing is to the Lord. The gospel was preached to both the Jews and the lost sheep of Israel. The record of Christ's ministry to the latter was kept from our knowledge because the gospel which was preached in Jerusalem was sufficient for the time. Once it became apparent to the heavenly Father that the deficiencies of the gospel would be discovered and become widely publicized, however, it was time for the revealment of the Nephite record. In it is found the fullness of the gospel. This is the future declaration that Jesus was to make. The word which he declared by mouth was rejected. In his death and resurrection it became the good news of the gospel. It is in this triple action—declaration to the Jews, to the lost sheep of Israel, and the revealment of the fullness of the gospel—that the name of the Father as love is now known. Much depends on the consecration of those called to share it with the world.

Jesus' Commentary on a Difficult Subject

The question of the lost sheep has always been a difficult subject for commentators. Worse than this is the limit Jesus puts on his personal appearance— to the house of Israel only (Matthew 15:23). Fortunately, when he visited the lost sheep in America he solved the problem by his statement on the subject. Speaking to the Nephites he said:

The Father having raised me up unto you first, and sent me to bless you, in turning away every one of you from his iniquities; and this because ye are the children of the covenant. And after that ye were blessed, then fulfilleth the Father the covenant which he made with Abraham, saying, In thy seed shall all the kindreds of the earth be blessed, unto the pouring out of the Holy Ghost through me upon the Gentiles, which blessing upon the Gentiles, shall make them mighty above all,

245

unto the scattering of my people, O house of Israel: and they shall be a scourge unto the people of this land. Nevertheless, when they shall have received the fullness of my gospel, then if they shall harden their hearts against me, I will return their iniquities upon their own heads, saith the Father.—III Nephi 9:64-66.

In making this statement Jesus was quoting from the covenant-blessing given to Abraham (Genesis 22:22) and saying how the promise was now being fulfilled in his personal presence. The Father raised Jesus from the dead and sent him to bless the Nephites (lost sheep of Israel). Then, after the Nephites were blessed, the Father was to bless the Gentiles. This, however, was to come through the pouring out of the Holy Ghost through Jesus, not through his personal presence. The latter is limited to Israel only. This is in agreement with Matthew 15:23.

The same quotation from Genesis is referred to by Peter and is recorded by Luke in Acts 3:25, 26. The similarities between the two are quite visible— but so also are the dissimilarities. Luke says, "Unto you first God, having raised up his Son Jesus, sent him to bless you." The Jews are the addressees in this case. The word "first" requires a second. The kindreds of the earth are mentioned, but not as recipients of a blessing. This may be inferred, but it is not stated. The whole message is directed to the Jews. Such is not the case in the Book of Mormon.

This verse is also confusing to the exegete in the *Interpreter's Bible*, but from a different angle than ours. The word "raised" perplexes him. "In this case," he writes, "should first be taken as an adjective agreeing with his servant, as in 26:23, where Christ is the first to rise from the dead, and in Colossians 1:18 where he's the first-born from the dead?" The

246

Book of Mormon account as given by Jesus is, "The Father having raised me up unto you first." His very presence here on this hemisphere could only be the result of the resurrection from the tomb in Jerusalem. Jesus was raised and sent to bless the lost sheep because they were the children of the covenant. Then, after the Nephites were blessed, the Gentiles were to be blessed by the outpouring of the Holy Ghost through Jesus. This blessing of the Gentiles made them powerful above all. Pentecost sent the apostles to the Gentile world. The Holy Ghost had been their making.

The Gentiles also are to be the recipient of the fullness of the gospel. Luke does not mention this; however, it could be inferred from the nineteenth verse of this chapter. The times of refreshing may be the restoration of the gospel. One thing is very clear, however, when the statement of Jesus is read. In case of rejection of the gospel, the Gentiles will find the same iniquities they heaped on Israel being returned to them. The fulfillment of this is very clear as we witness the struggles of the Western world—or perhaps I should say the industrialized world.

A tangled subject such as the lost sheep is not the creation of John's imagination; neither can its fulfillment in the Book of Mormon be attributed to Joseph Smith's speculations. Jesus is the author of both, and the resurrection is the pivot for his extended ministry to the Nephites and to the world through the fullness of the gospel.

When we consider the impact of the resurrection on the confusion or unbelief of the disciples we come to grips with the value of the sacrament of the Lord's

Supper. The immediate followers of the Lord left him forsaken after his trial and crucifixion. It is the resurrection which brought them together again. When they discovered that he was still alive his teachings, words, and commandments came alive also. After they had fished all night without any success and heard the voice of the stranger on shore saying, "Cast the net on the right side of the ship," and had caught many fish they recognized him as the risen Lord (John 21:1-9). It is here, after the resurrection was confirmed to them, that they recognized their unworthiness and his perfect holiness. In this setting Peter cried, "Depart from me; for I am a sinful man, Lord."[22] If we follow the account in John 21 we discover that Jesus broke bread with them. Many commentators look at this statement as reminding the disciples of the Lord's Supper—and probably it did. At that moment the impact of his example, his teachings, and his redemptive power began to take shape in their souls. This was what sent them into the world and obligated them to keep the covenant.

Fear that the evidence God gave regarding the divinity of Jesus in the Book of Mormon might not be true has contributed to erosion of the meaning of the Lord's Supper. This in turn has immobilized the missionary effort of the church and has impeded progress toward the cause of Zion. Perhaps—since confirmation of the resurrection of the Lord from the tomb in Jerusalem has been bolstered by the repeated evidence of the presence of "other sheep" from the house of Israel on the Western Hemisphere and of Christ's visit to them after the resurrection—this discovery will create in us a sense of guilt as it created in Peter and lead us to true repentance. The bread we eat and the wine we drink at the table of the Lord are not only memorials of his person but also reminders of his commandments and teachings. This is what we have covenanted to keep.

---

1. Matthew 28:1-14.
2. Mark 16:1-13.
3. *The Rise of Christianity*, p. 168.
4. I strongly suggest that those who have limited time, but want to pursue the subject further read the commentary in the *Interpreter's Bible* on Mark 16.
5. Luke 24.
6. John 20 and 21.
7. Matthew 27:3-10.
8. Zechariah 11:10-13.
9. I Corinthians 15:3-8.
10. Acts 9, 22, 26.
11. Acts 3:30, 31, 33, 38; 17:3, 18, 31; 23:6; 24:15, 21; 26:8, 23.
12. I Corinthians 15:37, 38.
13. II Corinthians 5:1-8.
14. II Corinthians 12:1-4.
15. John 10:16.
16. Matthew 15:23.
17. Matthew 10:4, 5.
18. III Nephi 5:8.
19. III Nephi 5:12.
20. John 12:28.
21. John 17:1.
22. The occasion which drew this sense of guilt from Peter was when he and his associates had fished all night and caught nothing. In the account reported by Luke (5:1-8) Jesus told Peter to "launch out into the deep." Then their fishing became successful. A comparable account is found in John 21. Some students feel that Luke and John were reporting the same event, but due to oral tradition Luke placed the event before the resurrection while John placed it after the resurrection. Considering, however, that John was an eyewitness to Jesus' ministry and Luke was not, and also considering the repeated harmony of John's account with that of the Book of Mormon, we must conclude that Luke's account misplaces the event (see *Interpreter's Bible* on John 21:4-9). Probably the confession was made as Luke recorded it, but John ignored it completely. Peter's repentance is known throughout the gospels, however.

CONCLUSIONS

It may have been observed from this study that the sacrament of the Lord's Supper was and still is the center of all Christian worship. Unfortunately, far too many have come to consider it as an isolated or a friendship meal, such as was customarily eaten on special occasions among the Jewish people. Because of the confusion over the Passover issue and the discovery of New Testament texts older than the King James, marked changes in the wording appear in relation to the establishment of the Lord's Supper. Some students attach no religious significance to it outside the memory of the Lord. Neither do they see any need for priesthood ministry in its observance. In contrast to this, the older Christian bodies look at it differently. They depend on tradition and the fourth century text of the New Testament. In the course of time the meal was surrounded with excessive pageantry and, in some cases, with absurd theological interpretations. This destroyed the simplicity and the efficacy of the Eucharist as intended by the Lord and observed by the apostolic church. Guided by the ministry of the Lord to the other sheep of the house of Israel, and by his observance of the meal and the instructions he left, the centrality and simplicity of the Lord's Supper are restored. Certain salient facts emerge which, as communicants, we need to be reminded of. They are:

1. *Deliverance.* The need for deliverance has always been associated with human beings. Whether they were in their primitive state, congregating along waterways and in forests, or living in the twentieth century, they felt their inability to deliver themselves from the environment, from themselves, and from their destiny. It may sound paradoxical, but during the last two hundred years, some scholars ignorantly began to ridicule the idea of deliverance. Now the scientific and technological discoveries in which we have trusted are posing a major threat to our survival. We are still, more than ever, crying for deliverance, for salvation.

2. *The Deliverer.* E. Stanley Jones once observed that there are two parallels in history: In one man cries for deliverance, and in the other—running close to it— the deliverer is provided. This is best seen in our civil and economic institutions. The Israelites experienced it when in Egyptian bondage. Any deliverance provided by man is subject to human flaws and frailties. At the sacrament of the Lord's Supper we see the infinite deliverer as the body of Christ is depicted in the symbols of bread and wine. These elements remind us of Jesus of Nazareth who came to earth, taught, suffered, and eventually was crucified but arose from the dead to become the savior of mankind. We do recognize him as our personal savior and deliverer.

3. *The Covenant.* Once deliverance is sought and the deliverer is found, an agreement, a contract, a covenant is made. On the grounds of faith in Christ and repentance of past attitudes and deeds, we penitent individuals went through the waters of baptism, making our covenant to serve him. This is a most solemn

rite, undertaken with utmost seriousness. Sins are remitted and we look forward to the observance of his commandments.

4. *The Commandments.* One of the many contributions Latter Day Saintism makes to Christian theology is the inclusion of the commandments in conjunction with the memory of the Lord. When the purpose of the Lord's Supper is limited to the remembrance of the Savior only, the tendency is to look to a past event. Once the commandments of the Lord are linked to his memory, however, the participant considers the past, revives action for the present, and looks forward to the establishment of Zion in the Hebraic sense or the kingdom of God in the Christian sense. This has been the aim of the Restoration from its beginning. At the Lord's Supper table we are individually and collectively involving ourselves in obedience to his commandments.

5. *Priestly Ministry.* This fundamental principle of the Christian system came up unexpectedly in our study. Its presence contradicts those who oppose priesthood as a special class in the church. Also, in function, it contradicts those who feel that priesthood is necessary in order to offer the sacrifice of the Mass. Both ignore its calling, teaching, preaching, and sacrificial shepherding function.[1] According to Matthew, Christ insisted that the eleven "teach them [those baptized] to observe all things whatsoever I have commanded you." Priestly calling obligates both the priest and the communicant. The writer of Hebrews defines the responsibility of the priest and lay member in this manner:

Obey them that have the rule over you, and submit yourselves;

252

for they watch for your souls, as they that must give account, that they may do it with joy, and not with grief; for that is unprofitable for you.[2]

Hence, the priest is a devotee of the new revelation of Christ. As a votary he studies the word as well as the needs of souls. Without deviation he administers the message with kindness, humility, and love.

6. *Agency.* Whether priesthood or laity, as participants in the sacred meal we cannot blame our failure to build the kingdom on anyone else, not even the devil. The inclination for good and evil are part of our creation. No man or devil can overpower us unless we allow ourselves to be enticed by their temptations. But there is one to entice us toward good deeds—the invisible Christ who is symbolized by the bread and wine of this sacrament. When the priest petitions the heavenly Father "to bless and sanctify this bread to the souls of those who partake of it," he does it in order "that they may eat in remembrance of the body of thy Son," and also that they may "keep his commandments which he has given them." The sanctified bread and wine are stimuli to the soul to sharpen its spiritual sight and quicken its kingdom-building activities.

7. *The Cross.* Those of us who share serious-mindedly in this meal recognize that our redemption comes through the cross. Consequently, it will be a cross that will take us to the goal. Jesus said, "Whosoever will save his life shall lose it; and whosoever will lose his life for my sake shall find it."[3] Neither the missionary nor the Zionic tasks can be accomplished without sacrifice and suffering. A thoughtful look at life shows it to be filled with suffering. Moments

of genuine well-being are few indeed. After considerable vacillation and trials the apostle Peter came to this conclusion: "For it is better, if the will of God be so, that ye suffer for well doing, than for evil doing."[4] At the holy banquet we dedicate ourselves to kingdom building, rather than perish with the kingdoms of man.

8. *Assistance.* As we strive toward the fulfillment of our convenantal pledge we have the promise of the Holy Spirit. This is an experience in which all the Saints have shared. A general definition falls short of its rational explanation. We best understand it when it fulfills our need as we try to make sainthood meaningful.

9. *Hope.* Three things made primitive Christianity dynamic and should make the church dynamic today— the cross, the resurrection, and Pentecost. The cross scattered the church. The resurrection brought it together. And Pentecost sent it in unity into the world. These three features are woven into the Lord's Supper experience today. Confusion over tradition, contradictions, and omissions in the New Testament account have scattered the church. The restoration of the gospel is intended to bring it together. In the process of this gathering, hardships and sacrifices are entailed. The aim may never be realized in our lifetime. But though we die short of the objective, we die with the conviction of ultimate victory. "If in this life only we have hope in Christ, we are of all men most miserable."[5]

10. *The Host.* The important thing to keep in mind is that we are guests at the Lord's table, and Christ is the host. The minister is simply his visible and

254

audible representative. The Lord, as symbolized in the bread and wine, is still presiding. This is best illustrated in his absence from the physical sight of his disciples in Palestine after the resurrection and his physical presence among the Nephites. We say that he ascended into heaven, but at that very same time he was physically visible to the lost sheep of the house of Israel. When, in his physical absence, the church in Palestine served the sacred meal, he was still with them through his Spirit. As a source of comfort, he told the twelve when he served the first Lord's Supper: "Yet a little while, and the world seeth me no more; but ye see me; because I live, ye shall live also." Most likely they did not understand what he meant. Even now its meaning may be obscure. What the Lord meant is that death could not annihilate him. Proof of this was his dual presence at the same time in Palestine and America. In Palestine he was spiritually present. In America, he was physically present. To the scoffers among the Jews and to the materialist of our day he was gone, completely destroyed. But to the apostolic and the primitive church, he was still present though invisible to the eye. He remains invisible, but—after this study—can we say that he was annihilated? Certainly not. He is present with his covenanting people and presides over his Supper.

In respect for his presence we are asked to kneel. This is the only prescribed ritual in the church, and it is not an empty one. We are dining at the table of the King of kings and Lord of lords. In his divine presence, what else can we do in appreciation of his love and atoning sacrifice but kneel?

Our posture is a simple expression of our sincere humility and determination to keep his commandments.

11. *Self-examination.* In the light of the foregoing, the advice of Paul to the Corinthian Church becomes more meaningful:

> But let a man examine himself, and so let him eat of that bread, and drink of that cup. For he that eateth and drinketh unworthily, eateth and drinketh damnation to himself, not discerning the Lord's body.

This advice is for the church of today. What do we see on and at the Lord's table? Are we discerning enough to sense his presence? An affirmative answer focuses our attention on his purpose in us.

In view of this study, I trust that the debate concerning the Passover issue is now settled. We know the Lord served the Supper on the day of preparation and near to the Passover. He may have had both in mind when he dined with the twelve. As the Jews set apart a day of preparation for the Passover feast, we as the Lord's covenanting people are to prepare ourselves spiritually for the Supper. We do this through self-examination to see whether we *discern his commandments* as we *discern his body.*

12. *Rewards and Penalties.* Every covenant has clauses detailing results of infraction of the agreement as well as benefits in case of compliance. This runs throughout the story of the Old Testament and the New. Perhaps it would be wise to review the account of the Sinai covenant. It served as a background for the teaching of the Lord. Moses read the law to the audience, and the people agreed to abide by what was read. "And he [Moses] took the book of the covenant, and read in the audience of the people:

256

and they said, All that the Lord hath said will we do, and be obedient." The same is required of the disciples of the Lord. Both John and the Book of Mormon insist on this obedience. The temptation to tamper with the instructions through rationalization or to ignore them will bring ill results. That is why Paul said, "For this cause many are weak and sickly among you, and many sleep." The worst that can happen to the church is to be a "sleeping" organization. Judgment can overtake it as a thief in the night.

Obedience to the commandments brings peace, and through the Holy Spirit we will experience unity with our Lord and with the heavenly Father. It is this unity which will bring needed love in the congregation and ultimately result in the establishment of Zion.

---

1. I may be accused of oversimplification of a very complex problem. This is not a treatise on priesthood.
2. Hebrews 13:17.
3. Matthew 16:25, K.J.
4. I Peter 3:17.
5. I Corinthians 15:19.

ABOUT THE AUTHOR

George A. Njeim, a minister for the Reorganized Church of Jesus Christ of Latter Day Saints for forty years and a former member of the council of Presidents of Seventy, was awarded his superannuation pin at the church's world conference in April 1970.

From 1967 until 1969 he was assigned to the West Central States Region. He was administrator of the Northern Plains and Prairie Provinces Region from 1964 until 1967, and his assignment from 1962 to 1964 took him to the Northwest Central States field. He also ministered in California and the Northwestern States, in Canada, in the Midwest, and in the East Central States. His first church appointment in 1930 was to the Toronto District.

Born of Lebanese parents in New Zealand, he was baptized a member of the Saints Church in Lebanon in the summer of 1914. For eight years he had no contact with the church. In 1923 he went to Jerusalem where the church was established and from the missionary there he gained valuable knowledge about the church which led him to come to the United States.

He studied at Graceland College, Lamoni, Iowa, for almost three years.

Mrs. Njeim, the former Vera Lillian Gamet (a graduate of the Independence Sanitarium and Hospital School of Nursing) died November 11, 1975. Their two daughters, Marie (Mrs. Michael Coulson) and Elizabeth (Mrs. Merle Maggard), live in Calgary, Alberta, Canada, and El Dorado, Kansas, respectively. George resides at the family home in Lawrence, Kansas. This is his third book. The others are *He Saw History in the Making* and *Insights into the Book of Revelation*.